Reviving Your Passion

DARRELL HUFFMAN

26 25 24 23 22 8 7 6 5 4 3 2 1

REVIVING YOUR PASSION

978-1-954966-99-4

Published by:
Emerge Publishing, LLC
9521 B Riverside parkway, Suite 243
Tulsa, OK 74137
Phone: 888.407.4447
www.emerge.pub

Library of Congress Cataloging-in-Publication Data:
ISBN: 978-1954966-12-3 Perfect Bound

Printed in the United States

Contents

PART ONE

REVIVING YOUR PASSION FOR GOD

As I was praying and getting ready for this message, the Lord spoke to me about four areas where people need revived. First, the people need to revive their passion for the Lord. Second, we need to have a reviving of the anointing of the Holy Spirit in and upon our life. Third, we need to revive and stir up our gifts and anointings that God has given us to use for His Kingdom. Finally, we need to have a reviving in our heart to win the world, to touch lives and bring people to Jesus. That is what we're going to deal with in this book.

We're going to begin with reviving our passion for the Lord, Jesus Christ. In Matthew 22, when the Lord was asked about the greatest commandment, He said that it's to love the Lord your God with all your heart, with all your soul, and with all your mind (see verses 34-40). That means there's effort involved. You are to be intentionally in love with God. That is where the Lord wants us to be.

As I was studying this out, the Lord really gave me David as an example. We all can probably relate to David. David was a man after God's own heart. He loved God, but David was far from perfect. In the Old Testament, you have two types: David's type and Daniel's type. Nobody can relate to Daniel because I don't think Daniel had a flaw. Daniel did everything right. Daniel never messed up. You never read about Daniel ever having a bad day. He lived an extraordinary life with the Lord.

Then we read about David. David is out here messing up, getting in places where he shouldn't be and having to repent and allow the Lord to straighten him up. But even with all of his flaws, David was one of the greatest kings, if not the greatest king, that ever lived because Jesus came through him. In fact, the Bible says that the Lord will sit on his father David's throne. Therefore, the kingdom was established through David and Jesus came to establish that kingdom to us. David would be all in serving the Lord and then he would get into trouble. Then David would have to be renewed and revived.

Some people might say if I talk about David like this, I'll give everybody a license to sin. But you'll sin enough without a license. I'm trying to give you a license to get out of sin, to get back with God so that you can live a life that is full of fire and faith and not let your mistakes mark you and determine who you are. Your passion for God and your dedication to the Lord is what should mark you. It is your desire to please Him and live for Him. It is you letting God do great things in your life even though you're a flawed individual. Many times as we try to teach faith, living for God and being righteous, everybody thinks you've got to be perfect. We strive for perfection, but none of us has made it yet. We have to get honest with ourselves, honest with the Word of God and realize that it is not by our might nor our power that we're going to get this thing done anyway. It is by the spirit of the living God and God's hand upon our lives that things are going to change.

As we begin to read in Psalm 100, it will begin to really set the place for us. It will begin to set us in God's attitude on how we're to live and serve Him, and how our lives are supposed to be.

In verse 1, David says, "Make a joyful shout to the Lord, all you lands!" (NKJV). The KJV says, "Make a joyful noise unto the

Lord, all ye lands." Notice David starts this song with saying make a joyful shout. We should have a joyful shout. Not just a shout, but a shout of praise, a shout of excitement, a shout of glory. He said it is for all you lands or all nations. Everybody should have a shout of joy and victory in their mouth. When it comes to the Lord, too many people are shouting at the Lord instead of shouting with joy to the Lord.

David goes on to say, "Serve the Lord with gladness; Come before His presence with singing" (Psalm 100:2 NKJV). I looked up that word "serve," and there are some different meanings in Hebrew. It can mean work, but another definition is worship. David was saying serving the Lord with gladness is your work and servanthood to the Lord is your act of worship. In other words, how I serve the Lord and the works I do for the Lord are an outward display of my worship to the Lord. Worshiping the Lord is not just singing; worshiping the Lord is my attitude toward the Lord. My actions toward the Lord and my service to the Lord become my act of worship to Him.

David goes on to say, "Know that the Lord, He is God; It is He who has made us, and not we ourselves; We are His people and the sheep of His pasture" (Psalm 100:3 NKJV). A lot of people don't know that the Lord is God because if we really had a revelation that "the Lord, He is God," we would act different. We would talk different. We would treat people different. Notice that he says you need to get the revelation that the Lord, He is God; He's not just a friend. He's not just a buddy. He's not just somebody you go to. He's someone you reverence and acknowledge as the Lord God Almighty every day of your life. Then he tells us that God made us. The Bible says in Ephesians 2:10 that "we are His workmanship, created in Christ Jesus for good works" (NKJV). The Lord is God, He created us, He oversees us and He's Lord over us. We need to have that revelation.

Verse four tells us, "Enter into His gates with thanksgiving, and into His courts with praise. Be thankful to Him, and bless His name" (Psalm 100:4 NKJV). The AMPC says to enter His gates as "a thank offering." I like that! I don't enter into His gates just saying thank you. I enter into His gates as a thankful offering. In other words, I'm the thank offering that's coming to Him. It's not just the words of my mouth, but the attitude of my life, my actions, who I am, all that I am. Everything in me is being presented to the Lord as a thank offering. He is receiving me, not just my words, as a thankful offering to the Lord.

Why should we be so thankful? Because Colossians 1:12-14 says we're to give "thanks to the Father who has qualified us to be partakers of the inheritance of the saints in the light. He has delivered us from the power of darkness and conveyed us into the kingdom of the Son of His love, in whom we have redemption through His blood, the forgiveness of sins" (NKJV). Why shouldn't we be a thank offering to the Lord?

On my worst day, I ought to be thanking God. I'm delivered from the power, the dominion, and the authority of darkness. God created me, He is my Lord. The devil may roar all he wants to, but I don't belong to him anymore. I listen to another voice.

David ends verse four with this: "Be thankful to Him, and bless His name" (Psalm 100:4 NKJV). He has said we need to enter God's gates with thanksgiving, go into His courts with praise, and be thankful to God and bless His name. These are three foundation statements that will help you to live a life that is full of revival, vigor, blessing, and excitement. David finishes the psalm with "For the Lord is good; His mercy is everlasting, And His truth endures to all generations" (Psalm 100:5 NKJV). John 17:17 says that God's Word is truth. The Lord is good, His mercy is everlasting, and His Word is truth to every generation. You have to know these three things about the Lord. But of all these three things, you first must know that the Lord is good. We serve a good God. His mercy endures and it is everlasting. His mercy is His willingness to get involved in our lives. His truth is for every generation.

The goodness of the Lord, the mercy of the Lord, and the truth of the Lord is for me in every situation in my life. That's how we're to serve the Lord, and that's how we're to live. We're to live with a thankful heart, we're to live with a shout of joy, we're to live and worship God and realize our service to the Lord is our act of worship that He sees. We're actually a thank offering to the Lord because we recognize that He is God and we are not. He created us for His purpose; and He has given us all these blessings. We can live with an attitude of victory because the Lord is merciful and the Lord is good. The Lord's truth is available to me in every situation I find myself in.

This truth is repeated in the New Testament. First Peter 2:9-10 says, "But you are a chosen generation, a royal priesthood, a holy nation, His own special people, that you may proclaim the praises of Him who called you out of darkness into His marvelous light; who once were not a people but are now the people of God, who had not obtained mercy but now have obtained mercy" (NKJV).

The apostle Peter is basically telling us the same thing that David said. God chose us before the foundations of the world; before there was ever a thing that was brought in, God chose you and me to be a part of His kingdom. When man messed up, God already had a plan that had been agreed on between Him and His Son, that He would send His Son to redeem us because God chose us. Once God has made up His mind; you can't talk Him out of it. You might ignore it. You might fight Him on it. You might run from it, but you can't change God's mind. He is going to chase you down. As long as you have breath in your lungs, He's going to do everything He can to get you delivered from sin. He's going to do everything He can to redeem your life and get you into His kingdom. That's how much God loves you and me. So quit fighting it or running from it and yield to God.

Peter tells us we are a chosen generation, His own special people. Why? Because the Lord made us, we're His own special people. You might wonder what you are supposed to do with that information. Peter tells us it is so "that you may proclaim the praises of Him who called you out of darkness into His marvelous light" (1 Peter 2:9 NKJV).

He's saying that once you recognize that God chose you and

drew you out of darkness, drew you out of the dominion of Satan, and brought you into His kingdom, redeemed you by the blood of the lamb and made you His own son, He also made you a royal priest. Now you can offer up spiritual sacrifices and praises to God. You can worship Him as a priest and you can minister. God has chosen you and brought you out of darkness and now God is saying, "Now I want you to proclaim, to demonstrate, to put out before the whole world your praises and all your attitudes of victory. Let everybody see that you're no longer a child of darkness. You are a child of light."

That's the way God wants us to live. Salvation is not a one-time trip to the altar and then you go live any way you want. That's not Christianity. That's not what it means to be a new creation. If you're going to become a part of the chosen generation, if you're going to become a part of the royal priesthood, and if you're going to come out of darkness, God is going to expect you to live in the light of who you are in Christ. God is going to expect you to come before His presence with singing. God is going to expect you to have a joyful shout of victory because you're no longer going to hell. Jesus is now your Lord, and your Father in heaven loves you. You've received the spirit of adoption. You cry out, "Abba, father." Your life is going to be lived as a thank offering to the Lord to bring praise and worship to Him. Your service is always going to be directed at Him. If I'm helping somebody, it's because I'm serving the Lord, and I'm doing it as a thank offering to the Lord. If I'm speaking a word of blessing to somebody, I'm doing it as a service to the Lord. In other words, I'm displaying and putting out before all that I am a child of light and not a child of darkness. I'm proclaiming it to the world so that the people can see what God has done in me.

He goes on to say we are a people "who once were not a people but are now the people of God, who had not obtained mercy but now have obtained mercy" (1 Peter 2:10 NKJV). I have obtained the mercy of God. First John 3:1 says, "Behold what manner of love the Father has bestowed on us, that we should be called children of God" (NKJV). In the fourth chapter, he says that right now in this lifetime, we are like Jesus. I've been created in His image. God has placed His Spirit in me, His anointing in me. His redemption is operating in my life, and now I'm to live as a child of light. I'm no longer a child of darkness. My attitude is an attitude of victory and blessing unto the Lord.

All these great truths are presented to us, and we are now to embrace them. We look at them. We say, "Glory to God. I will serve the Lord with gladness. The Lord is good. His mercy endures forever. His truth is to every generation." We say, "Oh thank you, Lord Jesus. I'm a child of God. I'm a chosen generation. I'm a royal priesthood. I'm going to shout the praises of Him who is drawing me out of darkness and has brought me into His light." We say, "I used to not be a part of the kingdom of God, but now I'm a part of the kingdom. And Jesus is my Lord."

Even though you have received this revelation and you have been saved, you feel the Spirit and you're excited about living for God, have you noticed that the world didn't change just because you did? There is still darkness out there, still temptations, tests, trials, tribulations, struggles, problems, and enemies attacking. You changed; the devil didn't and sin did not change. God changed you. He didn't change everything around you. When you got saved, you were still in the same environment you had been a few minutes before when you were lost. The devil still comes to steal, kill, and destroy.

That's why in Galatians 6:9, Paul says not to grow weary while you're doing the good things that God has called you to do because you will reap if you don't faint or get all fatigued and lose heart. In other words, you will have an opportunity to grow weary. Maybe you've realized that once you got saved, everything around you didn't get saved. All the people around you didn't get saved. Your circumstances didn't get saved. You just became the odd person out, and you recognize it.

If you get with a group of ten and you go out and wallow in the mud, walk in the trash, and do all this stuff, after a while, all ten of you stink. You all smell the same way, you look the same way, and you act the same way. Then you decide that you're going to go in the house and clean up. So you take all those clothes off, throw them away, get in the shower and scrub down, and you brush your teeth. You put some new clean clothes on, walk out and there are the other nine. You'd say, "Man, you guys stink."

They get mad at you for telling them they stink. You can't understand why they can't understand why they stink. But it is because they haven't been washed from the mud and the junk that's making them stink. They didn't change. You did. Now what the Lord wants you to do is to let them know what He's done for you, He'll do for them; that He can clean their lives up and give them a new life just like He gave you. To win your friends to Jesus, you can't go back into what the Lord has delivered you from. Your new life in Christ must become a greater influence to them than their life in sin is to you.

That is when the thief comes. He wants to come, break us and bring us down. The devil doesn't mind you going to heaven. He just minds you sharing heaven while you're on the way. He knows he can't stop you from getting to heaven if you make Jesus Lord. He's going to be out to stop you from living for God and letting people see what God can do for them while you're here on the earth.

We have to understand that there's a war going on. There's a battle. There are things that are going to attack us to try to pull our shout of joy away from us, to try to pull away our praise from God and to pull away the light shining out of us. There are things that are going to pull away from us an attitude of gratitude and a thankful heart and presenting ourselves as serving God as a thank offering.

So, what are you going to do? In Psalm 138, David says, "I will praise You with my whole heart; Before the gods I will sing praises to You" (v1 NKJV). In other words, you've got to get your heart into this thing. It can't just be a head thing; it has got to be a heart thing. If we're going to see God move in our time right now and see a great new revival come upon America, we're going to have to have some heart praise. We're going to have to have some heart living. In the second part of the verse, the word "gods" can also be magistrates or angels. So, David is saying, "I will praise you, Lord, before the demons of hell. I'll praise you before those that are in authority on the earth. And I'll praise you before the heavenly host." In other words, everywhere I am, no matter what I'm doing, my life is going to be a praise offering because my heart is praising God. I'm going to worship my God. I'm going to live a life of worship to my Lord.

He goes on to say, "I will worship toward Your holy temple, and praise Your name for Your lovingkindness and Your truth; for You have magnified Your word above all Your name" (Psalm 138:2 NKJV). We find that David is praising God with all of his heart. David is praising the Lord with passion and purpose. He's praising because he's magnified His name. He's glorified His name. I looked up the word "passionate," and it means you're having or showing strong feelings. When you hear somebody say, "I feel really strong about that," it means they are passionate about that. David was saying, "I want to praise you, Lord, with my whole heart." You should always be saying, "I'm going to praise You with a passionate heart. I'm going to praise You with strong feelings. I have strong feelings toward this." I have a conviction for this. I'm committed to this. I believe in this praise, God; this is how I'm going to live. This is what I'm going to do.

At the end of verse two, he says, "For You have magnified Your word above all Your name" (Psalm 138:2 NKJV). You might wonder how could God magnify His Word above His name? Throughout the Scriptures, there is no name greater than the name of the Lord. In Jesus' name, every knee will bow and every tongue must confess that Jesus is Lord (see Philippians 2:10-11). At the name of Jesus, every demon, everything has to surrender to the name of Jesus. Sickness flees at the name of Jesus. There's no name above the name of Jesus. How could David say He magnifies His Word above His name? He's saying your name is only as good as your word. The Lord is saying the reason the name of Jesus is so powerful is because He watches over His word to perform it. His word will never return to Him void. It will always do what it says.

What he's saying is, "When you begin to respect my word, what I say, and the integrity of my word, then the name of Jesus will become that much greater in your life because you understand that the name of Jesus represents everything God ever said." God is as good as His word. God's word is as good as God. God says, "The name is so strong and powerful because my word is backing it. My word can't be changed or altered."

So, we begin to worship God and stand on His Word. Now I'm serving Him and praising Him with my whole heart, but I'm serving Him and praising Him with my faith in His Word because I know His word is backing everything He said He would do for me. Now I'm committed to His Word.

In Psalm 138, David is worshiping God. He's getting a revelation of how great the word is and how good God is. Then he gets down in verse seven. He says, "Though I walk in the midst of trouble, You will revive me; You will stretch out Your hand against the wrath of my enemies, and Your right hand will save me" (Psalm 138:7 NKJV). It's similar to Psalm 23, when he wrote, "Yea, though I walk through the valley of the shadow of death, I will fear no evil" (v 4 NKJV). In other words, we're all going to have to walk through this valley of the shadow of death. The shadow of death is around us always because the law of sin and death is still in operation on the earth. The devil, who is the author of death, is still on the earth. Therefore, there's death, spiritual death and physical death, and struggles, problems, and troubles all around us. In fact, the word "trouble" here means to have adversity, affliction, and distress.

David is saying, "I'm walking in times of affliction, distress, struggle, and trouble. It's all around me. But you will revive me." He's saying, "You will quicken me, recover me, repair me, and restore me." That's what the Hebrew means. He says, "I'm walking in the midst of this and the enemy came in to pull me down. He came in to steal my joy, to get me away from God. God, in the midst of all that trouble, as I keep my eyes on you, you will revive me. You will quicken me. You will restore me and recover me. You'll bring into my life blessing and keep me alive."

The second half of the verse says, "You will stretch out Your hand against the wrath of my enemies, and Your right hand will save me" (Psalm 138:7 NKJV). In other words, "God, I allow you to keep me alive, keep my praise and keep my eyes on you. Every time the enemy tries to steal something out of me, you just revive it. Every time the enemy tries to pull me down, you restore me. Every time the enemy tries to get me to quit, you just go ahead and ignite and infuse me with your love."

David continues to praise after saying, "God, look, what's happening against me." He closes with this: "The Lord will perfect that which concerns me; Your mercy, O Lord, endures forever; Do not forsake the works of Your hands" (Psalm 138:8 NKJV). He's saying that you may find yourself in a time of trouble, distress, or affliction, or if you find yourself in a time when you just want to quit, you want to give up because you don't think it's worth it, and you don't even have a praise in your life and in your mouth, you just want to fuss. But David says, "Lord, in the midst of that trouble, you're going to stretch forth your hand and revive me, recover me, restore me, quicken me and infuse your life into me. Lord, instead of yielding to the trouble, the struggle, and letting it put my fire out, I'm going to let you perfect that which concerns me in this." In other words, "God, you're going to take what the devil meant for bad and turn it for my good. I'm coming out of this thing a whole lot better than I was when I went into it."

That's the attitude of Christianity. That's living Christianity. It's not Sunday morning religion. It's not a trip to the altar to get some fire insurance. We, as the church, have to come back to this place and realize that the reason I need to be revived is there's a bad world out here. The reason I need God to infuse life into me, restore me, quicken me, and keep pouring into me is because I've got troubles, struggles, and distress. These things are trying to zap everything out of me. But I didn't get into this thing just until the first struggle. I got into this thing to make it all the way to heaven. If we're going to go to heaven, we might as well enjoy the trip. How am I going to do that? I'm going to do that by letting the Lord revive me. I'll do that by letting the Lord restore me, quicken me, renew me, and bring His power into my life.

To see how you can do that, look at 1 Samuel 30. David has been out fighting his enemies and doing all this great stuff. He comes back to Ziklag, his home. The Amalekites showed up while he was gone. They burned the city, took his family, took his prosperity, took everything. He was devastated. This is David. This is God's man. This is God's king. He's already been anointed to be the next king. He's the one that Jesus is going to sit on his throne. He just had his family and his finances messed up. The enemy just came in like a flood while he was gone.

David and his mighty men reacted just like most of us: "Then David and the people who were with him lifted up their voices and wept, until they had no more power to weep" (1 Samuel 30:4 NKJV). When the enemy comes in and tries to pull the rug right out from under you or smack you down, and you find your head where your feet were, your feet where your head was and the whole world looks like it's turned upside down, it's okay to have emotions. They're weeping because they're upset. They're sad.

In fact, this next verse goes on and says this: "And David's two wives, Ahinoam the Jezreelitess, and Abigail the widow of Nabal the Carmelite, had been taken captive. Now David was greatly distressed, for the people spoke of stoning him, because the soul of all the people was grieved" (1 Samuel 30:5-6 NKJV). That word "grieve" means bitter. They weren't just upset. Now they're mad.

Here's a little history of this because this is a real good picture of the church. This is David and his mighty men. They've never lost a battle up to this point. This group got together when David went down to the cave of Adullam and the ones who showed up were his family, his own congregation. Then people started showing up: the discontented, those in distress, those in debt, those who were outcast, those who were struggling, those who were upset with the world. It sounds like when we came to God in debt, in distress, discontent, struggling, and with problems. These people showed up with David and from 1 Samuel 22 all the way to 30, they have victory after victory, after victory, after victory, and they turn into God's mighty men. They turn into covenant men of God. Their families are blessed. Their homes are blessed. They're beating everything they come up against, and God is prospering them. God is protecting them. God is taking care of them. All of a sudden, here comes this problem. The enemy comes in and he hits them like a snowstorm. He just falls on them like a flood. Now all of a sudden, the revival is over because here's some adversity.

The problem was that every one of them had forgotten what he said in Psalm 100, that the Lord is good. His mercy endures forever. And His word is everlasting to every generation. They forgot the Lord is good. They forgot that His mercy is everlasting, and they forgot that the truth endures to every generation. So, they weren't operating in His truth. They weren't operating in His mercy, and they don't think God is good anymore.

I don't care how great a revival is. There's going to come a day when the enemy is going to come in and attack it and see if he can break it down and destroy it. I don't care how great things are going on in your home, in your personal life, in your family. A day is coming when the thief is going to come in like a flood. He's going to come in, and he's going to try to steal, kill, and destroy. He's going to try and get you out of church. He's going to try and get you out of the intimacy that you have with God. He's going to try to steal your shout of joy. He's going to try to steal the thanksgiving out of your life. He's going to try to get you to quit serving God. He doesn't mind you going to church because you go and fuss at the pastor. You fuss at the person beside you. You fuss at your life and you've fussed at your family. Your thoughts are on what's going on, and all the time that the praise and worship is going on, you're just thinking about how bad things are. When the preaching is going on, you think, they've got to cut it back because if they preach too strong, you're going to get mad and get up and leave and whole groups will say, "Oh, we'll just get rid of that pastor."

David had changed the lives of this group. He's a man who has helped them to know God. Now they've set each other against him and they're mad at God because the enemy's come in. David begins to show us a few steps here on what we can do to take what the enemy meant for our bad and let God perfect that which concerns us.

Revival doesn't mean you're not going to have some problems next week. Revival doesn't mean you're not going to ever have another struggle or trouble. Revival means you keep yourself so in tune with God, so excited for God, so passionate about God that no matter what the devil throws at you, God's truth is going to be your truth. You're going to have God do a work in you. You're not going to let the enemy steal your walk with Jesus Christ. There are five things David did. The first thing is in verse 6: "Now David was greatly distressed, for the people spoke of stoning him, because the soul of all the people was grieved, every man for his sons and his daughters. But David strengthened himself in the Lord his God" (1 Samuel 30:6 NKJV). We all have to experience revival personally. Revival doesn't happen to a group. Revival happens to an individual, and all those letting God do a revival become a group.

Instead of responding to the struggle, responding to the anger, responding to the hurt, responding to the struggles and troubles, David goes back and practices what he spoke about in the Psalms. David goes to the Lord. Some translations say David encouraged himself in the Lord. David strengthened himself in God. David probably went to the Lord and said, "Lord, I don't know what I did, but I did something. And I ask you to forgive me. I repent. I repent for being aggravated. I repent for everything I've ever done. And, God, right now I don't know what to do. So, I'm just coming to you. I'm bringing my life to you because this is beyond me. I can't get out of this."

When you're under attack, that attack is going to run you from God or run you to God. We're going to have revival in the churches across this nation. We're going to begin to see all this stuff that is going on around us. We can't try to stick our head in the sand like an ostrich. It won't go away; it will pull on you and try to tear you down. You can let all the stuff that's going on around us make you run away from God and lose your joy, or it's going to cause you to run to God and begin to strengthen yourself in your walk with him. I choose to run to the Lord. I choose to be encouraged and strengthened in the Lord.

Look at the next thing it says in verse seven: "Then David said to Abiathar the priest, Ahimelech's son, 'Please bring the ephod here to me.' And Abiathar brought the ephod to David" (1 Samuel 30:7 NKJV). The ephod is a priestly robe. David was a king, but David knew right now that to have a move of God it wasn't going to come from him trying to be a king and a warrior; it was going to come by him being a worshiper, a praiser, and a priest to his God. There comes a point in time when we're going to have to take off our battle clothes and put on our priestly robe. We're going to have to begin to minister to the Lord and seek the Lord with all of our heart and realize we can't fight this in our own strength. We'll say, "I can't fight this enemy. I don't care how strong I am or how many Scriptures I can quote. I don't care how many years I've been in church. God, I am not able to overcome this. I need you." Revelation 1:6 says, Jesus "has made us kings and priests to His God and Father" (NKJV). You became a priest. David humbled himself to the Lord, David surrendered himself to the Lord, and he ministered to the Lord.

Then we find the second thing David did. David got himself in a place where he could hear from God. "So David inquired of the Lord, saying, 'Shall I pursue this troop? Shall I overtake them?'

"And He answered him, 'Pursue, for you shall surely overtake them and without fail recover all.'»

So, David went, he and the six hundred men who were with him, and came to the Brook Besor, where those who stayed were left behind. But David pursued, he and four hundred men" (1 Samuel 30:8-10 NKJV). Notice there are two things that go on here. First, David humbles himself. Second of all, David inquires of the Lord. David gets a word from God and believes he's heard from Him. He trusts his walk with the Lord, who says to pursue this. David doesn't just get a word and sit on it. David gathers his group together and starts acting upon it.

So, the first thing I have to do, if I'm going to have revival, is humble myself before the Lord. I'm going to have to realize I don't care how strong, how tough, and how bad I think I am. I'm going to put on the priestly robe and humble myself. I will submit myself to God and have an encounter with Jesus. Number two, I can't just assume that I can do this. I need to hear a fresh word from God. Once I'm hearing from God, I need to do it. That word is not going to do me any good if I don't act upon it. Then we pick up in verse 17: "Then David attacked them from twilight until the evening of the next day" (1 Samuel 30:17 NKJV). What a sign of revival this was. He's thinking, "I've humbled myself. I've encouraged myself in the Lord. I've gotten rid of everything. I've gotten rid of my hurts. I've gotten rid of my grief. I've gotten rid of my sadness. I've gotten rid of the things people said about me. I've gotten rid of the distress. I've gotten it off of me. I'm not condemning myself anymore. I don't care what anybody else does." David didn't go and ask the other people to come and get in the prayer closet with him. David just left them and got into it himself.

So whether anybody goes with me or not, I'm going to have revival. Then once I get myself where I've submitted myself and humbled myself to the Lord, I'm going to say, "Lord, I need a word from you. What do you want me to do?" Whenever I hear God speaking to me, I'm going to get up and I'm going to start doing it. It must have been a real strong passion. David must've got his passion back because all these guys that were talking about putting him to death are now jumping on the bandwagon and going with him. One believer full of revival, full of fire, and full of the anointing of the Holy Ghost can change an entire group of people that don't know God. God doesn't need a multitude. He needs one. He needs you and me.

David fought this enemy from sundown, basically, to sundown. He fought all day long until he finally conquered them. It can happen because you're experiencing revival. Because you've had a fresh anointing. You got a renewed word from God. You're not living on the word of faith that came to you back in the charismatic renewal. You can say, "God spoke to me today that He's my healer. God just spoke to me today. God just spoke to me again that He is my deliverer. God just spoke to me again that I can walk in His anointing. God just spoke to me that I can speak to the mountain." It's a fresh rhema word from God. You believe it so much that you begin to influence those around you. All of a sudden, they begin to see it.

But there's still an enemy out there that came in to stop this in the first place. You're all excited. You got a word, you rally the people, but you still don't have your family back. You still don't have your prosperity back. You still don't have all this stuff because the enemy has taken it. There's still a fight of faith that you're going to have to fight. You're going to still have to reassure yourself and take back what the enemy stole from you. You're going to have to defeat him because if you don't defeat the one who defeated you, he'll keep coming back and defeating you over and over again.

Revival isn't as a temporary fix. It's a change in life where you recognize the enemy. You recognize what he did. You recognize how he got in, and you go after him with all that's in you. You fight him and defeat him and bring him down. You want to revive your life. But every time you go ahead, that thing that's been coming at you knocks you back down again. You thought just because you got a fresh word that you were okay. But you are still going to have to go confront your enemy, and you're going to have to go after that enemy with a faith in God that cannot be shaken. David had six hundred men, and two hundred of them were so weakened and just depleted he had to leave them by the brook. Now he had four hundred and he had to go after this enemy that's undefeated. This enemy has beat down every town that they've gone to.

It sounds like what's going on in the world today. We've got a devil out there who stopped the Pentecostal movement. Then he stopped the healing movement. Then he stopped the charismatic.

Then he stopped the teaching movement, and he's been holding the churches' goods for several years.

You may have done great things in your past, but that enemy isn't going to get defeated because of the past or how many times you've been anointed in the spirit. You need a revival right now, renewal right now, a word right now, a new encounter with the Lord Jesus Christ. You need to humble yourself and seek God and then realize, "The reason the Lord is renewing me and giving me this word and making me an influencer is because there's an enemy out there that I'm going to have to fight. But this time I'll face it with a fire of God in my heart because God has magnified His word, even above His name. And I'm going after the devil with a word. I'm going after the devil with the name of Jesus. I'm going after the devil with the power of God. I'm going not because somebody else said it would work. I'm going because God spoke to me, and I know it'll work. I've gone before the Lord and encouraged myself and got washed by the blood of the Lamb, and all my sins, failures, and mistakes were cleansed. I no longer live in guilt or condemnation. I no longer live in inferiority. I'm no longer condemning myself and walking around in weakness. I had a new encounter with Jesus, and He's my Lord. He is good. And His mercy endures forever and His truth endures to every generation. I'm going to walk in the goodness of God, the mercy of God, and the truth of God. I'm overcoming this time." You gear yourself and you go.

The Bible says that David went in and he took back everything the enemy stole from him, plus the stuff they'd gotten from others (see 1 Samuel 30:19-20). When God begins to move in your life and you have a revival in your life, God does exceedingly, abundantly above all that you can ask or think according to His power that's at work in you (see Ephesians 3:20). God is a big God and a generous God. He'll do for you more than you thought you could ever believe God for. That's what He's wanting to do right now. God is wanting to renew our revival and restore to us even more than what the enemy took from us.

Even after this great victory David's mighty men tried to

immediately yield to the wrong spirit. I heard a story about a big revival where someone came in and barked like a dog. That's the only thing that people remembered about the whole service, that person barking. A pastor said, "Why would you stop a hundred people getting filled with the Holy Spirit to give attention to one person full of the devil?" He replied, "Our ushers, they're all trained. They took the dog barker and got him off in the corner. They cast that dog-barking demon out of him. Later on, he was praising God." Brother Hagan said, "Anytime there's a move of God, you're going to have a little fanaticism, a little crazy stuff." If you get filled with the Holy Ghost, and you have passion for God, not everybody's going to be happy.

We have to be alert to how the enemy does things. With David, they've had this great victory and God has done this great thing but immediately, the enemy is going to try to work. The men who fought the battle don't want to share the goods with the people that stayed with the supplies, so David calls them wicked men in verse 22. "But David said, 'My brethren, you shall not do so with what the Lord has given us, who has preserved us and delivered into our hand the troop that came against us. For who will heed you on this matter? But as his part is who goes down to the battle, so shall his part be who stays by the supplies; they shall share alike'" (1 Samuel 30:23-24 NKJV). He's saying God is good and it doesn't matter what's going on. Everybody's going to get in on it. We're not going to cheat anybody out of this thing. I shouldn't care if they're Episcopalian, Baptist or Charismatic, all are going to experience revival.

But it's going to start with each one of us. My question to you right now is this: What has your attention, the battles, the losses, the struggles, your failures, your war, or is it your relationship with Jesus? What direction are you going? Are you looking back to what you had and lost? Are you looking ahead to what God wants to give you? What's in your mouth? Are you fussing and complaining because you just don't see it and it's just not like it was? Or do you have a shout of joy and praise and thanksgiving to God? Revival starts with each and every one of us having a renewed encounter with Jesus Christ. That's where it starts. It doesn't start with me laying hands on people.

Remember that none of this started until David stepped out of the problem and stepped into the presence of God and rededicated himself to the Lord.

That's where the Lord will speak to us. Don't let your battles, don't let your losses, don't let what the enemy is doing or what's going on right now define who you are. Strengthen and encourage yourself in the Lord right now. Consider: Where am I at with Jesus? What's got my attention? What's got my voice? What's got my service? What's my attitude toward God? That's where revival starts: reviving something that was there, but has been lost. Renewing something that we'll see. Revival is God putting something new in; it's God renewing something that was already there. Revival is a fresh infusion. It's bringing back to life the things that have grown dead. It's being renewed with vigor and vitality in our attitude and service of the Lord.

PART TWO

REVIVING THE ANOINTING OF THE HOLY SPIRIT

Psalm 85:6-7: "Will You not revive us again, That Your people may rejoice in You? Show us Your mercy, Lord, And grant us Your salvation" (NKJV). When there's revival going on, people rejoice in the Lord. You can tell when there's a revival. There's rejoicing. If there's no revival, there's no rejoicing.

I looked up the word "revive" in the Greek, and it means to flourish anew. So, we can say, "Lord, will you not cause us to flourish again so we can praise you?" "Revival" in Webster's means restoration to vigor or activity. Lord, will you not restore us to vigor and great activity so we can praise you with our life? We can rejoice today that God is the God of praise. He's the God of worship. He's the God of revival. We believe that He's going to revive us. Christianity is not a Sunday morning religion, not a one-time trip to the altar. Becoming a new creation means that you are now changing lordship. You're coming from the kingdom of darkness into the kingdom of God. You're dedicating your life to be a light shining out to others. In fact, Christianity is serving the Lord.

We saw in Psalm 100, David said, "Make a joyful shout unto the Lord, all you lands! Serve the Lord with gladness" (v 1-2 NKJV).

We found that the word "serve" there means to work or worship. So, he said your service unto the Lord is your worship and everybody ought to have a shout of joy.

How would I know if I'm in revival? If I've been revived, I'm going to shout. I'm going to praise. I'm going to give praise to God and walk in His goodness. There's going to be a change taking place in my life. People should see revival in our lives.

David went on in Psalm 126 to say, "When the Lord brought back the captivity of Zion, We were like those who dream" (v 1 NKJV). When there's revival coming, when God begins to restore us and renew us and bring life back into us, we begin to dream again. We begin to worship again. We begin to shout praise to God again. We begin to live joyful lives. We rejoice with the Lord.

Then he says, "Then our mouth was filled with laughter" (Psalm 126:2 NKJV). If you got revival going on in your life, you're going to have some joy in your life. That frown is going to be turned back up again into smiles, laughter, joy, and rejoicing. And he goes on, "And our tongue with singing. Then they said among the nations, 'The Lord has done great things for them'" (Psalm 126:2 NKJV). Even unsaved people can see when there's a revival going on with God's people; it is noticeable to the world. We need to be living in such an anointing in the presence of God and with revival, restoration, renewal, and flourishing until the people around say, "The Lord is doing some good things for you; the Lord is blessing you." We're walking in that blessing.

We talked about serving the Lord in revival. It means that the church begins to serve the Lord. Our service to the Lord becomes an outflow of our relationship with the Lord if we're revived, we're full of the anointing, we're full of vigor, we're full of the rejoicing of the Lord, and we're flourishing in the Lord God. Whether you're in revival or you're not, our service to the Lord is always a reflection outwardly of what's going on inwardly in our lives. Therefore, we need to be in service for the Lord. We need to be excited for the Lord. We need to be full of praise to the Lord. We need to have songs of worship to the Lord. We need to live in such a way that, as 1 Peter 2:9-10 says, we are God's chosen generation and people know that God has brought us out of darkness and into His marvelous light. We're proclaiming that and living that and enjoying being a Christian.

Let us serve Him with gladness. The word "gladness" means mirth, merriment, and enjoyment. In other words, it ought to be fun being a Christian. We should be enjoying our trip to heaven. A lot of people have been saved. They're hanging on, holding out, and praying for God to come back again. But the Lord is saying to us that we should be enjoying this trip. We should be walking in His power, walking in His glory, walking in His victory. His presence should be in and upon our lives. We should be able to look at things and laugh. Not because you're disrespectful, but you're like Job. When he looked out and he saw destruction and famine, he said, "I'm just going to be like God. I'm just going to laugh. I'm just going to rejoice. I'm not going to let everything that's going on around me determine who I am. I'm going to let what's going on inside of me determine what I am and what I do and how I live."

That's where the church has to come to, a place of revival. Romans 12:11 says: "Never lag in zeal and in earnest endeavor; be aglow and burning with the Spirit, serving the Lord" (AMPC). Don't just go through the motions. Notice that he says be aglow and burning with the Holy Spirit, the anointing of God, serving the Lord. In other words, my service unto the Lord should be a passion. It should be aglow. I should be aglow. When I'm doing the things of God, I ought to light up. For you to be burning and aglow, you have to be filled with the Spirit. You have to be aglow and burning with the Spirit. You have to have the Spirit of God in operation in your life if you're going to serve the Lord with zeal.

The Message reads like this: "Don't burn out" (Romans 12:11). There's a lot of burned-out Christians today. Through attacks of the enemy, through discouragement, through some defeats in their life, through some failures, through something somebody's done to them, or some disappointment, they've gotten burned out or they tried to do too much too quick. They went way beyond their ability to believe God and just burned themselves out. So they decided, "It isn't going to work, so I'll just quit." But the Bible says, "Don't burn out; keep yourselves fueled and aflame. Be alert servants of the Master" (Romans 12:11-13 MSG). In other words, keep yourself fueled and aflame, that is important. In the Amplified, it says be aglow, burning with the spirit. The Message translation says, "keep yourselves." You have to take some responsibility to keep yourself fueled up and on fire for God.

That tells me if I have to keep myself fueled and aflame, that means I'm going to have to have constant, continual refreshing and renewing from the presence of the Lord. I can't live on yesterday's experience. Even in the Old Testament, when the children of Israel were in the wilderness, God rained down manna from heaven. They couldn't keep yesterday's manna in a container because worms ate it up. They had to go out every day and get new manna. God was telling them, "I want you to live for me every day of your life. I want you to trust in me every day of your life. I want to be your source every day of your life. I want to be the fuel that feeds your life and causes you to have strength and vigor to go on every day of your life. I want you to come out here and get some fresh manna from heaven every day of your life."

Paul is writing here to the church in Rome. He has brought us from the law into salvation by grace. He's brought us into the flow of the Holy Spirit, being led by the spirit of God. In Romans 12 he's talking to us about presenting our bodies, renewing our minds, realizing we all have giftings from God. Then he says, "Never lag in zeal and in earnest endeavor; be aglow and burning with the Spirit, serving the Lord" (Romans 12:11 AMPC). The Message translation says don't burn out with all this good stuff that God's doing in your life. Don't let it burn out. When you let a fire burn out, you quit putting stuff on it. You might have a great campfire going on, but if you don't keep tending to it, eventually it will burn out. You have to keep putting fuel on it. That's really what The Message Bible is telling us here. It's saying keep yourselves fueled and aflame. Keep doing what it takes to keep your fire for God operating consistently and continuously in your life.

After His resurrection, Jesus came in and taught the disciples until He was caught up to heaven. In the last days of His ministry, before He went on the cross, one of the most important topics that He would continuously bring up to the disciples was that they needed to get ready for another helper that was coming from heaven to help them to do His works and to serve Him.

In fact, even after He's raised from the dead in Luke 24, He basically tells them, "Now you've got to take this gospel to the world, you've got to bring them the message of remission of sins. Let people know that it's not a forgiveness of sins but a remitting of their sins. It's washing them and cleansing them in total deliverance from a sin life." He said, "Behold, I send the Promise of My Father upon you; but tarry in the city of Jerusalem until you are endued with power from on high" (Luke 24:49 NKJV). What he is telling us is for you to do this ministry and to serve me, I need to give you something that's going to help you to stay aglow, burning, on fire and not burning out.

After His resurrection as He is teaching on the kingdom in Acts 1, it says, "And being assembled together with them, He commanded them not to depart from Jerusalem, but wait for the Promise of the Father, 'which,' He said, 'you have heard from Me'" (v 4 NKJV). Notice He didn't highly suggest it. This is a commandment. This is an order from the commander in chief. This is the order from the King of Kings and Lord of Lords to those who are following Him. He commanded them, "The things I taught you before the cross—now you need to stay here in Jerusalem because it's about to come to pass."

He tells us what the promise is in verse five: "for John truly baptized with water, but you shall be baptized with the Holy Spirit not many days from now" (Acts 1:5 NKJV). Jesus was talking about the baptism of the Holy Spirit. He goes on to say, "But you shall receive power when the Holy Spirit has come upon you; and you shall be witnesses to Me in Jerusalem, and in all Judea and Samaria, and to the ends of the earth" (Acts 1:8 NKJV). The baptism of the Holy Spirit is not for their salvation. The baptism of the Holy Spirit is to empower them to witness and to bring salvation to others. He was not talking to them about them getting saved. He was talking about them receiving the baptism of the Holy Spirit. When they are baptized in the Holy Spirit, the Holy Spirit will come upon them and give them power, ability, efficiency, and might to go out and be a witness. The word "witness" here means one who can give evidence and proof of the resurrection of Jesus Christ. So, the baptism of the Holy Spirit is to equip us to serve God aglow and burning.

Next, let's consider what Peter teaches after the Holy Ghost is poured out and the anointing comes on him to begin to teach the Word. We need the Holy Ghost to come upon us. We need to have songs of praise. We need have rejoicing. We need to serve the Lord with gladness and mirth, and we need to have a shout of joy. We need to have laughter, and we need for people to see God working in our lives, but it cannot stop there. The power of the Holy Spirit is not just so we can be blessed. The power of the Holy Spirit is so we can take the zeal, the vigor, the excitement, the joy, the burning of God, and the passion of God out and win souls and bring people's lives to Jesus Christ.

Peter, on the day of Pentecost, was filled with the Holy Spirit. They were praising and worshiping God. But then all of a sudden, Peter began to preach. He took a text from Joel 2, and began to minister to them about what the Lord has done and what's going to happen in the last days. He talked about how Jesus is the Christ who God has raised up. In Acts 2:36, the Bible says this, "'Therefore let all the house of Israel know assuredly that God has made this Jesus, whom you crucified, both Lord and Christ'" (NKJV). When there is a real move and the Holy Spirit is being poured out upon people, we, as Christians, will begin to enjoy our trip on the way to heaven. But whenever we get out and begin to do the things of God, we will not draw attention to the Holy Spirit. We will not draw attention to speaking in tongues or the zeal, the laughter, and the joy. We will draw attention to Jesus Christ because the Holy Spirit came to witness and testify to the Lord Jesus Christ. True revival is going to bring a lot of people into the kingdom of God and help them to become servants of the most high God and change their lives.

Peter was preaching with boldness. When he got done, they asked the question that every one of us should ask, if we haven't already. "Now when they heard this, they were cut to the heart, and said to Peter and the rest of the apostles, 'Men and brethren, what shall we do?'" (Acts 2:37 NKJV). The difference in us trying to reach the world in our power as compared to reaching the world through the burning, the glowing, the power, and the anointing of the Holy Ghost is our words. In our strength, we do not have the ability or the power to cut into somebody's heart where they really need to be touched; I don't care how much you love Jesus. But words that are empowered by the Holy Spirit, words that are on fire with the life of God, flowing out of our lips, flowing out of us under the unction, the anointing, of the Holy Ghost: all of a sudden, they go beyond the flesh and they go down into the inner parts of the man. They begin to cut into the spirit of man, into the heart of man. All of a sudden conviction comes in and the question comes up, "Am I saved? And if I'm not, what do I need to do?" We need the Holy Spirit.

The apostle Peter begins to answer them, and there are some important points he makes. He taught them both the new birth and the fullness of the Holy Spirit: "Then Peter said to them, 'Repent, and let every one of you be baptized in the name of Jesus Christ for the remission of sins'" (Acts 2:38 NKJV). That's the new birth or repenting, which means turn your life to Christ, turn from doing it your way. "Repent" means an about face. It means to change what you think, change the way you live, change the way you believe, and turn to Christ. It also means to let the world know that you've turned to Christ by following Him in baptism, be buried with Christ, be raised with Christ, and live for Christ.

Also note that he didn't say forgiveness of sins. He said the complete blotting out and changing of your life, that you become a new creation in Christ Jesus. Your sins are remitted, never to be brought up again. Never to be thought about again. Nothing ever again to be said about them because the old man has passed away and all things have become new. A water baptism is you coming up out of that water saying, "I died with Christ. I was buried with Christ, and I'm raised up to live for Christ. And I want the world to know that I'm a new creation in Christ."

Peter preached salvation to them in the first part of this verse, but look what he says next: "'and you shall receive the gift of the Holy Spirit. For the promise is to you and to your children, and to all who are afar off, as many as the Lord our God will call'" (Acts 2:38-39 NKJV). He went back to the promise, saying the same thing Jesus said in Acts 1:4. Notice that God wants you saved by His Spirit, but He also wants you to receive the gift of the Holy Spirit and be empowered by the Holy Spirit. He wants you saved along with your kids, your grandkids, and your family. He wants everybody around you to be saved and filled with the Holy Ghost because you have turned yourself to God. He doesn't just want you experiencing this. He wants everybody to get in on this experience.

You might wonder, "How do you know he's talking about the baptism in the Holy Ghost?" Let's look at the word "gift" there again. You receive the gift of the Holy Spirit. Let's go over to Acts 10. Peter goes down to Cornelius' house and he begins to preach Christ to them. The Bible says, "While Peter was still speaking these words, the Holy Spirit fell upon all those who heard the word. And those of the circumcision who believed were astonished, as many as came with Peter, because the gift of the Holy Spirit had been poured out on the Gentiles also." (Acts 10:44-45 NKJV). The gift of the Holy Spirit had been poured out upon the Gentiles also. When the Holy Ghost came on them, "they heard them speak with tongues and magnify God. Can anyone forbid water, that these should not be baptized who have received the Holy Spirit just as we have?" (Acts 10:46-47 NKJV). He's talking about the baptism of the Holy Ghost. When you hear the teachers talking about the gift of the Holy Ghost, you know they're talking about the baptism of the Holy Spirit for the empowerment to be a witness for the Lord Jesus Christ.

Let's look at one more passage in Acts 11. Peter got called on the carpet up at Jerusalem for going down there and preaching to the Gentile "dogs." They called the Gentiles dogs. They thought we were the scourge of the earth. In fact, we were called common and unclean. But the apostle Peter had that vision while up on the housetop (see Acts 10:9-15) and the Lord spoke to him and said, "Don't you call anything that I've cleansed common anymore." When you've been cleansed by the blood of the Lamb, you're not common and you're not unclean. There isn't anything common or unclean about me. There isn't anything common or unclean about you. I've been washed in the blood of the Lamb and Jesus is my Lord.

Peter began to preach to them and he began to tell James what had gone on. He said this, "If therefore God gave them the same gift as He gave us when we believed on the Lord Jesus Christ, who was I that I could withstand God?" (Acts 11:17 NKJV). We find out that the baptism of the Holy Spirit is the gift of the Holy Spirit. That's how He's recognized. We find that out in Acts 10, ten to fifteen years after Pentecost, they got the same gift that the 120 got on the day of Pentecost. Acts 19 documents believers receiving the baptism of the Holy Spirit twenty to twenty-five years after Pentecost.

On June 7, 1977, at about twenty minutes to eight o'clock on a Tuesday night, I knelt down on the floor at my bedside in the upstairs bedroom of a farmhouse in Union Hall, Virginia. I asked the Holy Ghost to come in, and I got the same gift of the Holy Ghost that they got on the day of Pentecost. I got the same power. I got the same revelation. I got the same tongues. I got the same joy. I got the same victory.

That's where we've got to return. We've got to understand it's a gift, and the gift is given by the discretion of the giver. That means God chose. It's the promise of the Father. The Father chose to do this as His gift to His children. We have to serve the Lord aglow and burning with the Spirit. But if we're going to do that, we have to keep ourselves fueled and flamed.

Let's consider what's going to happen to you when you get filled with the Holy Ghost. Peter said the same thing that happened to the disciples happened to Cornelius. What happened to Peter is in Acts 2: "When the day of Pentecost had fully come, they were all with one accord in one place. And suddenly there came a sound from heaven as of a rushing, mighty wind, and it filled the whole house where they were sitting. Then there appeared to them divided tongues, as of fire, and one sat upon each of them. And they were all filled with the Holy Spirit and began to speak with other tongues, as the Spirit gave them utterance" (Acts 2:1-4 NKJV). But they didn't just speak in tongues. "And when this sound occurred, the multitude came together, and were confused, because everyone heard them speak in his own language. Then they were all amazed" (Acts 2:6-7 NKJV). People were amazed and started saying the Lord has done something great for them.

There's nothing common about the Holy Spirit. There will not be anything common about you and me. He's an uncommon gift. We are an uncommon people. We are a peculiar people. A God-chosen people. We're supposed to be letting our light shine unto Him. Look what happens then in verse 11: "'We hear them speaking in our own tongues the wonderful works of God'" (Acts 2:11 NKJV). The Holy Spirit was glorifying Jesus through the apostles. The Holy Spirit was anointing them to speak of the wonderful works of God.

Paul said in 1 Corinthians 12:3: "No one speaking by the Spirit of God calls Jesus accursed, and no one can say that Jesus is Lord except by the Holy Spirit" (NKJV). In other words, the Holy Ghost will never, ever bring anything but glory to the Lord. We should want to bring glory and speak of the wonderful works of God and let people see things in us and have a platform where we can speak boldly into them to get them to the place where they say, "What shall we do because our hearts are burning? At first, we thought you were strange. We heard you speaking in tongues. We saw you dancing and shouting and praising God. It seemed like you were just full of joy. We just couldn't understand it. But now that you've talked to us, what do I do to get this?" On that day three thousand came to Jesus Christ.

But we act like we don't need this today. When was the last time you heard that there was a crusade where three thousand people got saved? I believe we need revival. We need to be aglow and burning with the Holy Spirit, but we have to keep ourselves fueled.

David gives us some insight here in Psalm 92. He starts off by praising the Lord and exalting the Lord and magnifying the Lord. Then in verse eight, he says, "But you, Lord, are on high forevermore" (NKJV). He literally begins to exalt the Lord. He begins to magnify the Lord. Next, he says, "For behold, Your enemies, O Lord, For behold, Your enemies shall perish; All the workers of iniquity shall be scattered" (Psalm 92:9 NKJV). In other words, "Lord, I'm praising you and exalting you. And I believe that you're going to behold from heaven and you're going to work on my behalf and you're going to take care of my troubles."

He continues, "But my horn You have exalted like a wild ox; I have been anointed with fresh oil. My eye also has seen my desire on my enemies; My ears hear my desire on the wicked Who rise up against me. The righteous shall flourish like a palm tree" (Psalm 92:10-12 NKJV). Notice he started off praising God. Then he reminded Him of the enemies coming against him. But David believes that God is going to behold from heaven. He is not going to leave him and He's not going to forsake him. But he says, "Lord, I know I've got a part in this thing too. So, I'm going to ask you to exalt my horn like that of a wild ox."

Why the ox? When they were going across the Plains, they would get rid of the horse teams and give them a team of oxen. Horses would go out in that space where there was no water, it was hot and dry, and they'd wear out and wouldn't make the trip. They would put you in danger of dying. But an old team of oxen, you just give them a little sip every now and then give them a little bit of grain and they could walk you right across those plains. They were stronger. They were strong in themselves. David was saying, "Lord, make me strong. My horn represents my strength." The Amplified Classic puts it this way, "But my horn (emblem of excessive strength and stately grace) You have exalted like that of a wild ox" (Psalm 92:10). In other words, "God, I thank you today that you're going to give me excessive strength, more strength than I could ever need. And you're going to give me stately grace so I can stand in the midst of my enemies, carry myself with dignity and honor, and bring glory to you. Lord, I want to thank you right now that I'm anointed with the fresh oil of the Holy Ghost."

He said he's had the oil, but he gets some fresh oil now. I have to keep myself fueled and aflame. There is one baptism of the Holy Spirit for the believer, but there are many, many re-fillings of the Holy Spirit for the believer. Many times, we don't need another word. We need some fresh oil. We need a renewal. We need a reviving, a refreshing, we need God to pour His Spirit out upon us again. David says, "I'm anointed with fresh oil. Basically, I'm so anointed it just drips off of me."

That's why David said though we walk through the valley of the shadow of death, we will fear no evil. Wherever we walk, we're leaving a print. We're dripping with the oil of the Spirit. We're just staying full of the oil. Being anointed with fresh oil is kind of like a greased pig in a contest at a Fourth of July picnic. They used to have greased pig contests, where they would grease the pig to make him as slippery as could be. There was a big reward if you could go out and grab him, but nobody could grab him because he was so slippery. You couldn't keep hold of him and he'd get away. God is saying, "I want to anoint you with so much fresh oil that you just drip with the anointing of the Holy Ghost. When your enemies come against you, you're so full of the anointing that he may reach out and try to grab you, but he can't hang on to you. You walk in the power of God, and no weapon formed against you can prosper." You just stay aglow and walk in a stateliness, there's a strength about you, and there's a grace about you. People say, "That person must be a child of God because you can't act like that without God to help you. You can't be that calm without God's help. You can't have any joy without God in your life." We begin to be a demonstration of God's grace through the anointing of the Holy Spirit. We need a revival of the Holy Spirit.

In Ephesians 5, the apostle Paul is really giving us instruction on how to live for God, how to love God, and how to conduct ourselves. He says, "And do not be drunk with wine, in which is dissipation; but be filled with the Spirit" (v 18 NKJV). The Amplified Classic says it like this: "And do not get drunk with wine, for that is debauchery; but ever be filled and stimulated with the [Holy] Spirit" (Ephesians 5:18 AMPC). That's more accurate to the original Greek because it's to be ever filled; you could say it like this, but be continuously filled and stimulated.

The Greek scholars I've read say there's a play on words when he says, "but be filled with the Spirit." "Be filled" is a continuous action verb. He's not talking now about being baptized in the Holy Ghost when you go to God and confess Jesus as Lord. That's when you say, "Lord, I believe you now to fill me with the gift of the Holy Ghost. I'm going to receive the Holy Ghost coming into me, and as an act of my faith, I'm going to speak in tongues. I'm going to rejoice. I'm going to walk in the power of God. I receive the Holy Spirit as my helper right now." You receive that one time and the Holy Spirit comes into you and upon you, and you are baptized. He will never leave you nor forsake you. After you have been filled with the Holy Ghost and empowered with the Holy Ghost, you need continual refreshing and renewing and stirrings of the Holy Ghost in your life.

Revival is exactly what it says. Reviving what's in you. Restoring what's in you. If I get revived and I get re-filled with the Spirit, look what Paul goes on to say. "Speaking to one another in psalms and hymns and spiritual songs, singing and making melody in your heart to the Lord, giving thanks always for all things to God the Father in the name of our Lord Jesus Christ, submitting to one another in the fear of God" (Ephesians 5:19-21 NKJV). He's saying when you get a fresh anointing of the Holy Ghost, it's going to change how you talk, it's going to take doubt, fear, aggravation and frustration out of your mouth. You're going to begin to speak your faith. You're going to begin to speak joy, and you're going to begin to speak good things and blessings to people.

How do you know if you need a revival? What have you been talking? What has been the tone of your voice? What are you saying about yourself? What are you saying about our nation? What are you saying about your church? What are you saying about your family? What are you saying about your finances? What are you saying about your situation now? You need to be filled with the Holy Ghost and get the Holy Ghost back in your confession because the Holy Ghost speaks of the wonderful works of Jesus and the wonderful works of God. It'll change your attitude and praise. It won't be hard to get you to praise God. You'll begin to sing psalms and hymns and spiritual songs. The next thing you know, I've got a song in my heart. I've got the victory in my life. I'm praising God. I'm worshiping God. I'm magnifying God. I'm happy. When the enemy comes in, I'm like Paul and Silas, I pray, put it in God's hands, and start singing praise. I don't care if my feet are in shackles. I don't care if I'm in the back of the jail. I don't care if I've been beaten by the devil. I'm coming out of this because I'm full of the Holy Ghost, and you can't keep a revival man chained and locked up. He's got to come out. I've got praise in my mouth now and the Lord is on the throne of my life.

Paul also says to give thanks always for all things. Meaning I've got an attitude of gratitude. I'm serving the Lord with gladness. Paul also mentioned submitting, meaning it is not hard for me to submit to my God when I am filled with His Holy Ghost.

To know if you've got revival, first consider what's in your mouth. What are you talking about? What's your confession? Number two: Is there any praise in your mouth? Do you have a song of praise? Are you praising God in your situation? Are you complaining about your situation? Number three: Do you have an attitude of gladness, rejoicing, and shouting, and thanking

God right in the midst of your problem? Number four: Are you submitted to God and doing what He asked you to do? If you're not, you need to be revived and continually filled and you need to go ahead and fuel yourself up until your flames rise up again because these things happen when we receive a continual infilling and flowing of the Holy Spirit.

Now let me show you why we need this. In Acts 3, Peter and John go up to the temple and they get the lame man healed. Then they get to preaching and another five thousand people get saved through the power of God, the miracle-working power of the Holy Spirit. Peter said he could give the lame man what he had in the name of Jesus. He knew he had the name because Jesus had said, "You shall receive power, ability, efficiency after the Holy Ghost has come upon you, and you shall be my witness" (see Acts 1:8). The Holy Ghost lets you know who you are and what you have. The lame man began to walk, but Peter and John were taken and put in jail. It was already the evening, so they put them in jail till the next day.

In Acts 4:7-8, 10: "When they had set them in the midst, they asked, 'By what power or by what name have you done this?'

"Then Peter, filled with the Holy Spirit, said to them, 'Rulers of the people and elders of Israel: … let it be known to you all … that by the name of Jesus Christ of Nazareth … this man stands here before you whole'" (NKJV). This isn't the baptism of the Holy Ghost. Peter has already been filled with the Holy Ghost in Acts 2. He's not talking about getting baptized; he's talking about being ever filled and stimulated with the Holy Spirit. He's talking about receiving fresh oil of the Spirit of God. He's been empowered again with the Holy Ghost. In other words, the Holy Ghost came on him to restrengthen him and renew him for this moment. He declared that it is by the name of Jesus Christ that this man stands here whole and healed. He told them that at the name of Jesus, you'll get saved and there's no other name under heaven that you can be saved by because Jesus is Lord. He preached a powerful message because he got a refilling of the Holy Ghost. It revived the power of God in him.

"Now when they saw the boldness of Peter and John, and perceived that they were uneducated and untrained men, they marveled. And they realized that they had been with Jesus" (Acts 4:13 NKJV). Realize, they didn't have a doctorate degree from the seminary and no master's degree from the Institute of Sadducees. We need to be revived with the power of the Holy Spirit because we need the world to see that we've been with Jesus. How we handle things, our attitude toward dealing with problems and dealing with things, coming up with the right answers, and saying the right things in the right situations: that's what the Holy Spirit does. That's why the church needs Him so bad. That's why each one of us needs a fresh anointing of the Holy Spirit coming upon us.

The rulers told Peter and John not to preach in that name and then let them go. But Peter and John said they couldn't help but speak of what they knew. They went back to the church and began to pray and look to God. They began to report the greatness of God and all the good things of God. Then they began to cry out to God. Here's how they finished it in verse 29: "Now Lord, look on their threats, and grant to Your servants that with all boldness, they may speak Your word, by stretching out Your hand to heal, and that signs and wonders may be done through the name of Your holy Servant Jesus" (Acts 4:29-30 NKJV). Remember what David said in Psalm 92: "For behold, Your enemies, O Lord, For behold Your enemies shall perish; All the workers of iniquity shall be scattered" (v 9 NKJV).

Back in Acts 4: "And when they had prayed, the place where they were assembled together was shaken; and they were all filled with the Holy Spirit, and they spoke the word of God with boldness" (v 31 NKJV). This was the whole church in Jerusalem. This was a part of that three thousand and now five thousand folks. When they got saved back in the day, they got them filled immediately. They didn't just let them go about their business. They got saved, filled with the Holy Ghost, baptized in water, and planted in the church. Acts 2 says that the people broke bread daily. They lived for God daily. They came to the church daily. They fellowshipped daily. They read the things of God and lived on the doctrine of the apostles and they had great favor with the people. They were adding to the church daily as many as were being saved because they were full of the Holy Ghost. The Holy Ghost was making them witnesses, and people were recognizing Jesus in their lives. So, they had already been baptized in the Holy Spirit, but it says they were filled with the Holy Spirit. That means a fresh anointing of the Holy Ghost came upon the entire church. They all left that service speaking the Word of God with boldness and courage. The Holy Spirit is here to give us boldness and courage, to stand up against the attacks of the enemy and proclaim the goodness of God.

If you don't know Jesus yet, you need to receive the gift of salvation because that's God's gift to the world. Titus 3 says you receive salvation through the washing of regeneration and the renewing of the Holy Spirit (see v 5). In John 3, Jesus told Nicodemus that you must be born again: "That which is born of the flesh is flesh, and that which is born of the Spirit is spirit" (v 6 NKJV). In other words, your spirit man needs to be born of the spirit of God. You need to be born again. You need to receive Jesus Christ as Lord. You need to receive the gift of salvation because the gift of salvation is God's gift to the sinner.

Once you've made Jesus your Lord, you're no longer uncommon or unclean. Now you are a son of God, a daughter of God, a child of God. In Luke and also in Matthew, Jesus talked about how that if earthly fathers know how to give good things to their children, how much more will your heavenly Father give good things, the Holy Spirit, to His children? The Holy Spirit is God's gift to the church. The new birth is God's gift to the world, but the baptism of the Holy Spirit is God's gift to His people. That gift is to empower us and strengthen us to live our lives as a light shining out to others

Just because you get filled with the Holy Ghost doesn't mean you're not going to have struggles. Paul and Silas were beaten and thrown in jail, but they didn't get the Holy Spirit thrown out of them. In fact, they took Him to jail with them. You will face troubles and struggles. That's why the Bible says in The Message Bible, "Don't burn out." If you don't keep getting fresh anointings from God, your fire will burn out. You need to keep yourself fueled and aflame serving God in the Spirit.

How is your fire? We need to get some oil poured on our fire. You know what happens whenever you fill a lamp up with oil and put a match to it. If you don't have any oil, you can turn that little wick raiser on the old lanterns all you want, but it won't matter even If you had a wick, there isn't anything going to shine out of that lamp with no oil. But if you put oil back in the lamp and strike a match, then you could turn the wick raiser. It would just soak up the oil until all of a sudden, the flame would grow. That thing would light up the whole house because it was fueled.

With those old lanterns, you had to keep refilling them because you burned them up as you went about. Life burns up some stuff in us. That's why the Bible talks about being ever filled and stimulated with the Holy Spirit. That's why Paul told the Ephesian church to stay full of the Holy Spirit, constantly be filled and stimulated and stirred with the Holy Spirit.

Revelation 2 tells us what happened to the church of Ephesus. They didn't keep themselves stirred up. They didn't stay filled with the Holy Spirit. John writes a letter by the spirit of God to them and says, "You have left your first love" (Revelation 2:4 NKJV). They got religious. They lost their fire. They didn't do what Paul told them to do by the unction of the Holy Ghost. They didn't stay fueled and aflame. They let it burn out.

How much oil is in your lamp? I'm going to share with you what you need to do to be so full of oil that you have enough to pour out to somebody else. In John 7, Jesus said, "If anyone thirsts, let him come to Me and drink" (v 37 NKJV). I pray that I've made you so thirsty. You know the saying, "You can lead a horse to water, but you can't make him drink." My friend's daddy would say, "Yeah, but if you put enough salt on his tongue, the horse will drink water." I pray I've put enough salt on your tongue that you want to come and get a drink because that's what you need.

In fact, if there's something in you right now starting to resist and trying to get you to pull back, that's an indication you really need what I have shared. You need it. I need it. We all need it. If the body of Christ in America, or in any nation in the world, is going to have revival, we're going to have to see people hungry for God's Spirit, God's anointing, and God's power. We need a fresh anointing of the Holy Ghost.

PART THREE

REVIVING YOUR GIFTS AND TALENTS

I hope you are being revived and stirred by the spirit of God. That's what God wants to do for us. "To revive" in Greek means to flourish anew. It means you're flourishing. It's a new time. It's just like spring has just sprung up inside of you again. Webster says "to revive" means to return to life or consciousness. A conscious awareness of God's plans and purposes coming to life in me. It means a return to health or vigor, to come and bring back into use. That means that you did it once, but you let it slip away. To revive something means to bring it back to life. It means to bring it back into your consciousness, bring it back to where it's an exciting thing. Not just a mundane or ritual thing.

"Revival" in the Webster's says a reviving or being revived, a restoration to vigor, or activity. Meaning if I get revived, I'm not going to be able to just sit and watch everybody else do something for God; I'm going to be excited, wanting to do something myself. We're going to get involved and we're going to put our hand toward what God's called us to do.

We started in Psalm 100, where David said, "Make a joyful shout to the Lord, all you lands! Serve the Lord with gladness;

Come before His presence with singing" (v 1-2 NKJV). Revival is not just a feel-good service. The church has to have this revival and renewal in us. Salvation is not a trip to the altar. Salvation is not a Sunday morning religion. Salvation isn't to get saved and sit down and hang on till you get to heaven someday. Salvation and becoming a new creation mean that you become a servant of the Lord Jesus Christ. It means that you come into the kingdom of God and you give your life to Christ. Now you choose to grow in Him and you choose to be renewed in Him. You choose to let your light shine out to others. Every Christian should have a joyful shout of praise because of what God's done in their life. In other words, he's saying you want to be bold and just praise God almost all day. I've got a shout. I don't care who hears me. In fact, I want everybody to hear me because I've got a joy in my life that cannot be stolen from me because it didn't come from me. It came from Jesus.

Then he says in verse two to serve the Lord with gladness. In the Hebrew, the word "glad" means to serve Him with glee, joyfulness, mirth, or rejoicing. That word "serve" can also be translated to work for the Lord. It also is translated worship. That means your service to the Lord is your act of worship unto the Lord. Worship is not just us coming to church and singing. Our worship is demonstrated and on display every day as we serve the Lord in our actions and our deeds, our attitudes, our talk, and our walk. People see Jesus Christ in us. When you serve the Lord, what he is saying is, your worship goes way beyond the sanctuary walls. Your worship is a part of your lifestyle. Your worship is your service unto the Lord. Your worship is your dedication to Christ. Your worship is living the new creation every day of your life.

We begin to see these things, and we begin to thank God for these things. We begin to praise Him. David says in verse four to enter into His gates with thanksgiving. We saw that the word is a thank offering or thankfulness. We find out here that our service unto the Lord is worship, and then we're to come into His presence as a thank offering. It's not just our words thanking Him, but our attitude is thanking Him. Our actions, our attitude, everything about us becomes a thank offering to the Lord. I am His offering. Not just my words. I'm a worship unto the Lord. So, I begin to serve Him.

We looked at how we had to revive our passion to serve the Lord. We have to renew ourselves, and revival begins with me. It doesn't begin with us. You have got to put the me in revival before you can put the us in revival because every one of us individually must have an experience of revival in our own life. I need to be revived in my personal passion for the Lord. I need to be revived in my personal service unto the Lord. I need to be revived and come alive and stirred in myself to serve the Lord. Whenever I've got it operating in me, it is going to spread to others because fire begets fire. Instead of looking at somebody else and trying to make them get in revival, we should take a quick look at ourselves and say, "Lord, send revival to me. Stir me up in my service to you. Stir me up in my worship to you. Stir me up in my attitudes toward you. Lord, stir me up and bring alive in me a passion to live for you every day of my life."

In Romans 12:11, we found out, "Never lag in zeal and in earnest endeavor; be aglow and burning with the Spirit, serving the Lord" (AMPC). We need to be revived in the anointing of the Holy Ghost upon our life. The Message said, "Don't burn out. Keep yourselves fueled and aflame." In other words, I need to keep the fuel in there. I need to keep the oil in there.

We found out that we all need to be filled with the Holy Ghost. We need to have the gift of the Holy Ghost and be empowered of God and walk in the power of the anointing of the Holy Spirit. There's one baptism in the Holy Spirit and there are multiple refillings of the Holy Spirit, and we're to be continually filled and stimulated and stirred and anointed by the Spirit of God. In Ephesians 5:18, Paul says, "Be not drunk with wine, wherein is excess; but be filled with the Spirit" (KJV). That word "filled" there in the Greek means to be filled or stimulated and stirred or continuously filled with the Spirit.

That's not talking about filling up a glass of water until it just comes to the top. It's talking about the sail on a boat. When the wind catches that sail and fills it up, it pulls that boat right across the waves. When we get so full of the Holy Ghost, He's like the wind blowing from God. He catches our sails. When our sail gets so full, it just lifts us over top of the waves and it takes us to our destination. It's no more a struggle, but it is now us just cutting through those waves, enjoying the blessings of the Lord. I found out a few years ago when you have a motor on a boat, that motor drives that thing through the waves. It powers itself through the waves. But when you're on a sailboat, the sailboat doesn't power through the waves. The wind catches that sail and it just skirts over top of the waves. What Paul is saying is instead of trying to plow through the waves of life, instead of trying to plow through all the struggles of life, why don't you just go ahead and get filled with the Holy Ghost and let Him just fill you up to go over the bumps? He just pulls you right over top of the struggles of life and takes you to your destination without your effort, but His effort. The motor has to power the boat if it's the one that's churning through the water, but the person that's on the sailboat just sits there and lets the wind do all the work for him. It's not by might nor by power, but it's by the spirit of God that we're to get these things done.

In this part of the book, we're going to look at Ephesians 2. We're going to re-dig some wells. We're going to revive some things in our lives. We're going to unclog some streams that used to flow. We're going to restore some wells that once were producing blessing to people, but we allowed the enemy to come in and clog them up. Sometimes we kind of let those wells go because of disappointments or people discouraging us. Sometimes we just let them go dormant. We just let them burn out. We don't keep fuel in them. Therefore, we stopped doing the things that God called us to do and using the things that God called us to use. But in Ephesians 2:8-10, Paul wrote, "For by grace you have been saved through faith, and that not of yourselves; it is the gift of God, not of works, lest anyone should boast. For we are His workmanship, created in Christ Jesus for good works, which God prepared beforehand that we should walk in them" (NKJV). You always need to read verse ten with verses eight and nine. We have a bad habit of reading verses eight and nine that say by grace through faith and it's not of yourselves; it's the gift of God, not of works. God did a work in you, but why did God do a work in you?

The Amplified brings verse 10 out like this: "For we are God's [own] handiwork (His workmanship), recreated in Christ Jesus" (Ephesians 2:10 AMPC). I've been recreated. God came in, and the new birth means He took the old heart out and put a new heart in. God recreated me. He took me from a sinner to a saint. He took me from a dark and defeated sin-ridden devilish person and brought me over into the light. He recreated me, totally redid me. Why did he do that? He says we are "(his workmanship), recreated in Christ Jesus, [born anew] that we may do those good works which God predestined (planned beforehand) for us [taking paths which he prepared ahead of time], that we should walk in them" (Ephesians 2:10 AMPC).

He's saying the reason you got saved by grace and God poured out His Spirit and He reached down and redid you is because He had a plan for your life. With the plan for your life, He has works or service that He wants you to do for Him. Serve the Lord with gladness. That's a theme throughout the Scriptures. So, He recreated us by His grace and mercy in Christ Jesus. When He brings us into Christ Jesus, all of a sudden, He begins to declare to us and reveal to us, "I did this because I have a lifestyle I want you to live, works and deeds and things that I have created for you, things you are uniquely made to be able to do." We're a new creation in Christ Jesus, recreated in Christ Jesus.

But according to the Word, God recreates us in the image He wants us to be. Not everybody's made exactly the same. Not everybody has the same thing. Paul wrote to the Corinthians and said some of you are eyes, some of you are ears, some of you are hands, some of you are feet, some of you are mouths, but we're all the body. Every one of us is uniquely made to do something special in the kingdom of God. God had a plan of work for you, a planned operation for you, a life for you to live.

The end of verse 10 in the Amplified further explains the paths God prepared: "we should walk in them [living the good life, which he prearranged and made ready for us to live]." He calls it the good life. If you want to find joy and happiness and victory in your life, find out why God made you, find out what God made you to do, find out what God has put in you, and find out the life God wants you to live. Then jump in it with all you've got and start doing everything within you to serve God in the way He wanted you to serve him.

There's no greater joy. No wonder David can say to make a joyful shout unto the Lord. His whole heart was to serve God. He wasn't perfect. But at the same time, the Bible says that David was a man after God's own heart. He wanted to live and do and be what God created him to be. The Bible says that's what we're created for; God recreated us in Christ Jesus to do these things. When there's a revival going on, people are excited about what God wants them to do. People are looking for ways to serve the Lord. I like what Charles Finney said about revival. He said, "Revival is a renewed conviction of sin and repentance, followed by an intense desire to live in obedience to God." Charles Finney was a great revivalist, and he said revival is a renewed conviction of sin and repentance. In other words, it's a renewed conviction that I don't want to live in sin. I'm going to repent. I'm turning from sin. It is not going to dominate my life. That's followed by an intense desire to live in obedience to God. I have an intense desire to live in God's perfect will. I want to be where God is doing what God wants me to do. I want to walk under His shadow. It's a passion to serve the Lord. And remember being passionate means having or showing strong feelings. In other words, if I'm passionately desiring and intensely desiring the things of God, it means I feel strongly about this. If I'm passionate about something, I'm intense about it. At the drop of a hat, we'll talk about Jesus.

Paul said in Ephesians 2, we have to get into these works.

In Ephesians 4:1, the apostle Paul continues on and he says, "I, therefore, the prisoner of the Lord, beseech you to walk worthy of the calling with which you were called" (NKJV). He begins by saying that he has just totally locked himself up with the Lord. "I'm a prisoner of the Lord. I came in, locked myself in, and threw the key away. Don't try to get me out. I'm enjoying it too much. Don't try to set me free. I don't want to be free because I am free. The closer I get to the Lord, the more I enjoy the life He created for me."

Then in the second part of the verse, notice that every born-again child of God has a calling, or the King James says a vocation, an invitation from God to do something in the kingdom and in the body of Christ. Every one of us is called. You might be thinking, "Well, I just thought he was called if he was an apostle, prophet, evangelist, pastor, and teacher." But Paul didn't say in Ephesians 2:8 that by grace, every apostle, prophet, evangelist, pastor, and teacher was saved. He said that every person on earth is receiving grace and every person comes into a place where God has a work and a plan and a purpose for their life.

And now in Ephesians 4, he said for every believer, everyone who reveals themselves to the Lord, has a calling, an invitation, a vocation for you to live for Him and do something for Him. It's special. What should you do about your vocation and your calling? You should be like the apostle Paul, who said to the Romans, "I'm an apostle to the Gentiles. I magnify my office." You'll want to say, "I'm excited about what God called me to do. I put great stock in what God called me to do. I count it as a precious thing."

Then Paul says, here's how you're supposed to live, "with all lowliness and gentleness, with longsuffering, bearing with one another in love" (Ephesians 4:2 NKJV). He is saying there are a lot of people who are going to try to get you out of walking out your calling. You better stay humble. You better have some gentleness about you and meekness, and you better be long suffering. Long suffering, meaning long tempered and not easily roused, not easily upset, not easily defeated, not easily offended, not easily discouraged. I'm going to walk that way in my calling.

"There is one body and one Spirit, just as you were called in one hope of your calling; one Lord, one faith, one baptism; one God and Father of all, who is above all, and through all, and in you all. But to each one of us grace was given according to the measure of Christ's gift" (Ephesians 4:4-7 NKJV). He's talking to each one of us. I'm included in that. You're included in that. Notice with your calling and the work and the position and the thing that God has invited you to do when He recreated you, He's not only called you to do it, but He gives you the grace to be able to do it. Grace always comes with a call. Grace is God's divine influence and favor. In other words, he says, "I'm going to give you the grace, the divine influence and favor, to fulfill everything I've called you to do because it's not by your might or your power that you go and get it done. It's you walking in my grace, in my influence, in my favor, in my goodness, into my mercy and my presence in your life."

Then Paul goes on and he says, "Therefore He says, 'When he ascended on high, He led captivity captive And gave gifts to men'" (Ephesians 4:8 NKJV). Notice this third thing is that he gives you a gift. This word "gift" here means a supernatural endowment. He's not talking now just about the apostle, prophet, evangelist, pastor, and teacher, because he just said, "unto each and every one of us has given." So, every born-again believer reading this right now, every one of us, you need to understand: God saved you. God brought you into a work that He had already prearranged for you to walk in. And when you choose to walk in His plan and His purpose and do His work and serve Him with your life, it is a good life that He prepared for you to live. With the calling that He puts upon you, He gives you His grace and divine influence and favor to carry it out. Then God comes along and gives you a gift, a supernatural, spiritual endowment, something that's a talent, gift, and ability within you to do what you're called to do.

For there to be revival in the church, each and every one of us must come before the Lord as a believer and say, "Lord, I'm going to be revived in my calling that you call me to do, and I'm going to let you revive, restore, bring back to vigor and back to life and give me your grace." In fact, the apostle Paul wrote to the Corinthians and said, "By the grace of God I am what I am, and His grace toward me was not in vain; but I labored more abundantly than they all, yet not I, but the grace of God which was with me" (1 Corinthians 15:10 NKJV). The reason Paul did great things was this: Paul learned how to get it out of himself and get it over where God was taking care of him.

God is calling us now, and God is giving us grace now. God gives us a gift, a spiritual endowment so that we can walk and do the things that He's called us to do, but He doesn't stop there. "For I say, through the grace given to me, to everyone who is among you, not to think of himself more highly than he ought to think" (Romans 12:3 NKJV). Notice that Paul is telling everybody, "I'm operating in the grace. I'm doing the things that God called me to do, and I'm not doing it through my own strength." If you're doing it through your own strength, you're probably worn out, defeated, and need revival. You're trying to fulfill what God called you to do in your own intelligence, in your own mind, your own power. You are probably a burned-out vessel. But that's all right. We're going to pour some oil on you in this book. We're going to re-dig some of those things and revive them and bring them back to life.

Paul is writing to the church. He's writing to every one among them, every believer in the church at Rome, warning them all "not to think of himself more highly than he ought to think, but to think soberly, as God has dealt to each one a measure of faith" (Romans 12:3 NKJV). We have found out: God saved you by His grace. God has called you into His works. God prepared works for you to do, prepared a place for you to serve Him. God called you into that service. God gives you grace to do that service. God gives you the gifting of supernatural, spiritual endowments and abilities within you to do what He's asking you to do. Then he says He gives you faith so that you can make it work in your life.

I'm called. I'm gifted. I'm graced. And I've got faith to get it all done. You might say, "I wish I could have faith." Then get saved, because you can't be saved without faith because by faith you're saved by grace. Therefore, if you're saved, God gave you faith when you got saved.

Many walk around letting the devil think for them. The devil will try to control what you think and what you say. Don't let him control what you think or say; cast those things down and fix your mind on the Lord Jesus Christ. Set yourself to think like God wants you to think and believe like God. I believe that I'm born again. I'm a child of God. I'm delivered from the power of darkness, brought into the kingdom of the Son of God. God prearranged a work for me before He ever called me into salvation. Before I ever listened to Him, God had a plan for my life. God called me into it. He gave me a vocation with that plan. He gave me a grace to fulfill that vocation. He gave me a gift that I could operate in that would give me the strength to get it done. Then He gave me faith to make it work in my life. That's who you are. You may not know it yet, but just think on it a little while. It'll come to you. That's who you are. That's the new creation Christ made you to be. It's what God did in you when He recreated you in Christ Jesus.

Now look what Paul goes on and says you're supposed to do with that grace, that gift, that calling, and that faith. He says, "For as we have many members in one body, but all the members do not have the same function, so we, being many, are one body in Christ, and individually members of one another" (Romans 12:4-5 NKJV). We all have different functions and we're all different parts, but we're all the body of Christ. This confirms that we were all not created just exactly alike. We were all created in Christ Jesus, but God created us with a special uniqueness about us. You have a unique calling on your life. You have a unique grace in your life. You have a unique gift in your life. You have a uniqueness of faith in your life. There's something about you that makes you special. Wherever God wants you and He puts you in His body, you fit right in there. And when you fit in or you make it full, it makes it look good and it becomes a good life because now God is working through you. The vine is now pumping everything right into you as its branch. You have begun to walk in the things of God, and now the body's coming together and revivals are taking place because we're all serving the Lord with gladness and worshiping Him.

Let's go on to look at some of these different functions, gifts, special endowments, giftings, and abilities and talents. My gift might not be like yours and yours may not be like mine, but each one of them is unique and special in the eyes of God. "Having then gifts differing according to the grace that is given to us" (Romans 12:6 NKJV). In other words, I have grace for my gift. I don't have grace for your gift.

That's why some of us got burned out because we wanted to do what we were watching somebody else do. But God didn't call us to do that. God didn't create us to do that. God called us to do something else, created us to do something else, gave us grace to do that, and gave us faith to do that. But we wanted to do what they were doing. Therefore, we didn't have the grace to do what they were doing because the grace goes with the gift. So, if I want to walk in God's grace, I have got to get in my gift. I have to get in my place because that's where it's going to function for me.

He continues: "Having then gifts differing according to the grace that is given to us, let us use them: if prophecy, let us prophesy in proportion to our faith; or ministry, let us use it in our ministering; he who teaches, in teaching; he who exhorts, in exhortation; he who gives, with liberality; he who leads, with diligence; he who shows mercy, with cheerfulness" (Romans 12:6-8 NKJV). He is saying let us operate in those gifts. Let us use them for the glory of God. We could say, let us use them to serve the Lord with gladness.

There are different giftings in the church. Let's break them down. There's a difference in prophecy and a prophet's ministry. A lot of people see prophecy and they think they're supposed to go around and foretell and speak things over people. But that's not what he's talking about. Prophecy, according to 1 Corinthians 14:3, is edification, exhortation, and comfort. In fact, Revelation 19:10 says that the testimony of Jesus is the spirit of prophecy. Prophesying is according to the proportion of your faith. That means God will work in your life and you'll speak into people edification and encouragement and comfort, and you'll minister to them and you'll witness to them about Jesus. When you begin to talk about Jesus and you begin to speak out blessings to people, a spirit of prophecy comes on you and the anointing comes on you. It just begins to bless the people around you. Paul said all may prophecy that all may be edified. Some will do it more than others because you may have that uniqueness about you. When you begin to speak, there's an anointing that comes on you to be a blessing and an encouragement to people and to comfort people and strengthen them. God just gives you the words to say to them. It will be like when you walk off, you think, "Ooh, that was good. Where did that came from?" You won't have to wonder anymore. It didn't come from you, it came from God, who used you to be a blessing in that situation.

Also, he talks about ministry or service. It would be actually helps or supportive ministries. In other words, wait on your ministry, find out where you can support, find out where you can help, find out where you can get involved, and find out where you can serve God in the church.

Then he talks about teaching. That could be a traveling teacher, like one of the five-fold ministry. That could be teaching in Sunday school or youth teaching or in a Bible study teaching. In other words, it's bringing forth information and inspiration and revelation to people. There are people who have a gift of teaching. That doesn't mean they're going to be out ministering all over the world, but it means that God uses them to bring information and teaching. It just seems like it flows out of them. If you're not a teacher, don't try to be a teacher. Just like if you're not a singer, don't try to be a singer. When it comes to teaching, not everybody is anointed to teach, but everybody can share and encourage and strengthen and share good news with others. But some are really called to teach and be a good teacher.

The word exhort means to encourage. When you get around people who are exhorters, they begin talking to you and you just feel good about yourself. You just feel like you can run through a troop when you get done talking to them because they're encouraging you. They're exhorting you to go on. When you get to them, they're just kind of stirring you up. If you've got that gift, you should use it for the Lord.

Then he talks about the giver. God blessed some people to be able to make money, more than most of us can make. But He expects them to be generous with that, giving into the kingdom of God, and they become supporters and financial givers and strengtheners into the body of Christ.

There are those who lead, all leadership: elders, team captains, department leaders. Paul says people who take the lead need to do it with diligence. In other words, if I'm going to take a lead role in some area, I'm going to be diligent and I'm going to do it out of the gift and the grace of God that's within me. I will serve the Lord with my gift.

Actually, there are acts of mercy and kindness. This would be a good visitation ministry. Those who are filled with mercy and kindness and cheerful when they go do it. When somebody is in the hospital, you don't want somebody coming in to say, "It looks like you're going to die. Let me pray. They told me it was bad, but I didn't know it was this bad. Oh God, Jesus help them now." You really don't want somebody showing up like that in your room. Those who show mercy and those who can come in and praise God, they can bring kindness and love and encouragement to you and lift you up and be there to assist you and bless you. When they leave, you just feel good because they loved you and they came to care for you and to minister to you and reach out to you.

What's exciting about this is that each one of these things Paul talks about is just as important as standing in the pulpit preaching because each one of these gifts are created by God, on purpose uniquely for that individual. That means God puts great stock in what He put in you, He puts great honor in what He created you to be and what He called you to do. A lot of us get out of that because we get burned out trying to use our gift and maybe somebody rejected it. We got discouraged a few times, or sometimes we just don't keep it fired up and inflamed. We forget what we were called to do. He says not to burn out, but keep fueled up and keep your flame burning.

In 1 Peter 4:7, the apostle says it like this: "But the end of all things is at hand; therefore, be serious and watchful in your prayers" (NKJV). Get serious about living for God. Get serious in your prayers. He adds, "And above all things have fervent love for one another, for 'love will cover a multitude of sins'" (1 Peter 4:8 NKJV). Love will cover a multitude of sins, both yours and theirs. Love will help you not be judgmental, burn out, grow weary or defeated. Love will help you to look beyond their faults and still want to minister to them. It will help you to do what God called you to do.

"As each one has received a gift, minister to one another, as good stewards of the manifold grace of God" (1 Peter 4:10 NKJV). Notice that each one has received a gift; the Amplified says, "As each of you has received a gift (a particular spiritual talent, a gracious divine endowment)" (AMPC). That's what that gift is, a particular spiritual talent, a gracious divine endowment. Then he tells us what to do with that gracious endowment. We are to minister to one another to be stewards of God's grace.

Then he adds, "If anyone speaks, let him speak as the oracles of God. If anyone ministers, let him do it as with the ability which God supplies, that in all things God may be glorified through Jesus Christ, to whom belong the glory and the dominion forever and ever. Amen" (1 Peter 4:11 NKJV). When he says the oracles of God, that means as a voice speaking out for God. He's saying when you are using your gifts, you're bringing glory to God.

Revival means more than just going to church. Revival is whenever you have an intense, burning desire to locate your place, your gifts, your anointings, your faith and grace and talents. You begin to cherish them. And you begin to say, "Lord, here am I. Send me."

If you go back and study the prophet Isaiah, he was looking

out and he was saying woe is this and woe is this. Woe are they. Then he saw the Lord in Isaiah 6, and he said, "Woe is me." All of a sudden, he realized he needed a touch. God sent an angel, who took the coal fire and touched Isaiah's lips to cleanse him. Then the Lord said, "Who will go?" And Isaiah replied, "Send me."

When you let God touch you, you want to be the one who gets sent. You want to be used of God. There's an intense desire that begins to rise up on the inside of you saying, "Lord, let me be used of you. No matter what it is, Lord, if it's being in the back with the kids and nobody will ever know it. You'll know it. I'll do it as unto the Lord with the gifting, the gracing of God, that that will bring glory to you and change my life and touch somebody's heart and raise a child for the kingdom of God. Lord, if it's out here working, if it's doing menial things that the world or that even the church says, 'Well, that's nothing much.' Lord, I'm going to do it with all my might. All my power. I'm going to do it unto your glory because I was uniquely made and qualified and created by you to do this very thing." That's revival.

Now let's look at how we are going to get there by seeing what Paul wrote to Timothy. Paul reminds him about his faith legacy. He says, "When I called to remembrance the genuine faith that is in you, which dwelt first in your grandmother Lois and your mother Eunice, and I am persuaded is in you also. Therefore, I remind you to stir up the gift of God, which is in you through the laying on of my hands. For God has not given us a spirit of fear, but of power and of love and of a sound mind" (2 Timothy 1:5-7 NKJV).

Paul is saying, "I know you have faith. I see the faith, but right now you're a little burned out and you don't even see your faith. You don't know what God's done in your past; you've forgotten where God has brought you from. You forgot what God has done to you. Now what you need to do is quit walking around here in this weariness and tiredness and wondering whether God loves you anymore or not. Realize you have faith, you have a gift, and you have an anointing. It's up to you now to stir that up and strengthen that and get it back alive in you and begin to do again what God called you to do." Paul is encouraging his spiritual son to get involved. I like what the Amplified says in verse six: "That is why I would remind you to stir up (rekindle the embers of, fan the flame of, and keep burning) the [gracious] gift of God, [the inner fire] that is in you by the means of the laying on of my hands" (2 Timothy 1:6 AMPC). Paul is saying, "Man, you need to fan the flame." Like he said in Romans 12:11 to keep the flame burning and stay aglow.

If we're going to have revival, we all need to stop for a moment and say, "Lord, what have I been called to do? What's my gifting? What's my grace?" When I find out what my vocation is, my place, my call and what God created me to do in my path, the lane I'm to run in, doing the work that I'm supposed to do. I'll find the people I'm supposed to influence and touch and bless, the things I'm supposed to do to make the kingdom of God come alive, the things I am supposed to do to help the church, reach the community, and do the things it's called to do. When I find that, then I'll understand that I have grace to help me to fulfill my call. I need to find that grace, that divine favor and divine influence from God to be able to do it, not in my own strength or power, but in God's ability and in His strength that He gives me. I've got gifts and talents that I've just laid down, but He helped me to bring them back alive again.

We need to say, "Lord, I'm going to stir up my faith and fan the flame. I'm going to get that fire burning again. I'm not just going to sit anymore. I'm not going to just shout anymore, I'm going to shout with a voice of triumph. I'm not just going to pray. I'm going to get serious in prayer. God, I'm not just going to go through the motions. In fact, if I find myself falling back in that lane of just going through the motions, I'm going to stir myself. I'll say, 'Stop it. I don't live like this. I don't live mundane Christianity. I don't live in defeat. I don't live in doubt. I don't live in fear. I don't live in timidity. I am a child of God. I've been recreated in Christ Jesus for good works. I've got a gift and I've got a calling and I've got grace and I've got faith and God's using me, and I'm going to do my part to bring the kingdom of God into this world. I know I've touched people's lives.'"

You're not going to get a new gift. When you got called, God gave you all He's going to give you. You can develop the gift, just like you can develop the grace. You're not going to get any more faith. God gave you a measure of faith, but you can develop that faith. When you were born and brought into this world, you had the same amount of muscle that you have right now. You haven't received any more muscles as you got older and a little stronger. Hopefully, you've made them a little bit bigger, but they're the same muscles you were born with. You don't get new muscles, but you can renew those muscles. You can strengthen them if you put them through the right situations. Your spirit, your gift, your call, your grace, your faith, your knowing: it's all given to you. God says, "Now you make it happen."

In Matthew 25 is the parable of the talents. Jesus told the story of the master who gave one servant five talents, one got two, and one servant got one talent. The one who had five went out and doubled them up. The servant with two, he went out and put them to use and they doubled up. If you use it, it increases. But one servant decided, "No, I don't think I want to do this." He put his talent in the ground. The only thing the Lord comes back and sees is his one talent.

God gives us talents and abilities and expects us to use them. When we use them, He increases them. He grows them. You get better at what you're doing. Some of us have taken our talents and we quit growing them. We quit using them. We buried them. But they only grow if you use them. What we've got to do right now is make up our mind that we're going to grow our talents and abilities. Everything has to come from your heart.

Timothy had quit serving God out of a passion in his heart and was serving Him out of his head and out of a routine. That's why his faith wasn't working. That's why his gift wasn't working. That's why he wasn't seeing results because Christianity became normal to him. It became common to him and he was living out of the natural instead of the spiritual. But Paul tells him to fan the inner flame, the fire of the Holy Ghost on the inside of him.

Pastors, Evangelists, Teachers, if we're going to preach, we're going to have to preach out of the heart. We can't preach out of memory. We can't preach out of what was; we can't preach out of what we've heard. Before we preach it, we need to dig back down in the Scriptures and make those truths come alive again, make those messages come alive again so that when we preach, it is flowing out of our hearts. It's like manna falling from heaven: revelation knowledge, not just knowledge.

Worship leaders, we cannot just have good songs. We have to worship out of the heart. We have to get before God in our praise so it is flowing up out of our heart and we're drawing people to the Lord.

Greeters don't just greet and be cheerful and just think you're showing up doing something for God. We should be thinking, "God, I'm going to change somebody's life today. God, I'm going to influence somebody for Jesus. God, somebody will come in here and they're going to need a handshake. They're going to need a smile. They're going to be blessed when they get into the sanctuary because, God, you created me for this. I have an anointing for this. And I'm doing it from my heart."

This starts coming when we're serving the Lord out of our heart and not out of our head. It releases the fire of God and revival breaks loose because when I'm serving God, I know why I'm doing it. I know the cause. If you don't know the cause or why you're doing what you're doing, you need to revive that fire because we've got to serve God from the heart. Revival begins in my heart; those gifts, callings, grace, and faith come alive in my heart. All of a sudden, I know what I'm here for. I know why I'm doing this. It's to glorify my Lord and touch somebody's life. It's to release His glory into this place and let Jesus be exalted and magnified in all of our lives. That's revival. God is looking for us to have that revival. I was praying about this, and I said, "Lord, how do you want us to stir these things up?"

The Lord said, "Did you notice that last verse you read where Paul said, 'the gift that you received by the laying on of my hands'?" I said, "Yes, sir." He said, "If Paul laid hands on him to get the gift, you could lay hands on them to help them to stir up the gift." Maybe you want to find someone to lay hands on you to help you get the gift. But if you don't have someone to do that, you need to stir yourself.

But this is the beginning. This is not the end. This is the start. This is us stirring ourselves. This is our gift, our passion for our service for the Lord and loving Him individually. This is our passion to be filled with the Holy Spirit and walking in the anointing of God. This is our passion to stir up our calling and our purpose in our calls in the kingdom again and know who we are in Christ.

I believe you're like me. I want to see revival more than I want to see anything else on this earth right now. I want to experience the glory of God. I want to experience lives being changed and multitudes coming into the kingdom of God. I want to experience healings and miracles and signs and wonders. I want to see people eager to get to church. I want to see people showing up early and praying and getting ready for a move of God. I want to see the areas across this nation talking about Jesus: "Did you hear what went on at that church Sunday? Oh, have you seen what was going on? Did you see what happened to so-and-so?" and talking about the Lord. I'm dreaming of it. I'm craving it and I'm hungry for it and I'm praying for it to happen.

We have to come back to the heart, just like Paul told Timothy, "Son, you've got to go back and remember what God called you to do, what He gave you faith for, and stir that inner flame. Get that fire burning again. Get that passion going again." I urge you to know your call, know your purpose, and let the anointing begin to rise up in you again. Whatever you do, do all for the glory of the Lord.

PART FOUR

REVIVING YOUR PASSION FOR THE HARVEST

We've talked about revival, which means to flourish anew, to be awakened. One translator said it means to return to life or consciousness. In other words, you're conscious of the presence of God again. The life of God is flowing into you again to return you to health or vigor, to come or to bring something back into use. You had it before, but you let it go dormant or you let it dry out or you let it burn out. But reviving means it's brought back to use again. It's working in your life again. God's doing something in you.

Revival means restoration to vigor or activity. God says when revival hits, He'll put a shout back in your shout. He'll put praise back in your praise; He'll put dance back in your dance. He'll put faith back in your faith because, all of a sudden, you're not just going through religious motions. It is a living, vital aspect of your life that God is real in your life. You're connected and united to the living God. We need to have revival. We need to have passion. The dictionary says passion or to be passionate means having or showing strong feelings. When there is revival going on, people have strong feelings and they show them. When was the last time that you just had a laughter come on you, that you were just happy about it? When was the last time you got in the presence of God and felt tears going down your face, and all of a sudden, the feelings and the emotions are stirred up on the inside of you and you just realize how much you love the Lord?

Any relationship that just has a legal love is a cold, dry relationship. It really has to go beyond just a legal love. It has to go into an intimate love and expressive love. We're not to just have a legalistic love for God and a walk with God, but we're to have an emotional, expressive, intimate relationship with God that just shows up in our life. It stirs our feelings. It gives us passion for what we do. It calls us to work with a vigor in our lives, with a zeal in our lives. We're stirred to do the things that God has called us to do. We've seen that you have to serve the Lord with gladness. We have to serve Him with that attitude and stir ourselves up. Then we found out that we need to have a fresh anointing of the Holy Spirit. We've learned we've got to stir up our gifts.

I was asked how you'd know what your gift is. One of my patent answers has always been this: when you're seeking the Lord and all of a sudden down on the inside of you, you see things that you enjoy doing and things you're good at that bless people; normally that's the gift that God placed in your heart. Some people say, "I'm concerned if I pray and ask God for a gift, He might give me something I don't want to do." Your gifting is something that you're going to enjoy doing, something you can excel at, something that you can be a blessing with, and something you can develop and mature in. That's how you discover your gift. When you spend time delighting and worshiping the Lord, God places in you the desire that's pleasing to Him, but also, it's pleasing to you (see Psalm 37:4-5).

We have found revival cannot just be contained and stay inside the church walls. For there to be a true revival, that fire has to break out of the sanctuary and flow out into the highways and byways and touch people's lives and change the culture of the nation that we're living in. The Bible says in the Old Testament that when the righteous are in authority, the city is blessed (see Proverbs 29:2). When we begin to walk in our authority and walk in the power of God, the anointing of God, God will bless the place.

Joseph walked in continual revival with the Lord and intimacy with the Lord, even though he was done wrong over and over and over again. Everywhere they put Joseph, God just prospered him. He was sold into slavery, to Potiphar, and his master became a wealthy man. When Potiphar blew it, they put Joseph in jail and the jailer was relieved to have him. The prisoners were happier with Joseph in charge. Finally, Pharaoh got wise enough to bring Joseph in. Egypt became the greatest nation on the planet because God moved. When there's a righteous person walking in the fire and the anointing of God, who has an intimacy with God and knows his authority, God can bless the whole area. That's why the Lord put us here. He put us here to be salt and light shining out into the world so that we can bring blessing and do away with the curse.

First Peter 2:9-10 tells us more about who we are: "But you are a chosen generation, a royal priesthood, a holy nation, His own special people, that you may proclaim the praises of Him who called you out of darkness into His marvelous light; who once were not a people but are now the people of God, who had not obtained mercy but now have obtained mercy" (NKJV).

Notice we are not just a priesthood, we're a royal priesthood. We're kings and priests unto our God. Revelation 1 says God has washed us in the blood of His lamb and made us kings and priests (see v 5-6). We're a royal priesthood that can offer up spiritual sacrifices and praises unto our God. We're a holy nation, not an unholy nation, not a religious nation, but a holy nation of people who live and conduct themselves in holiness and righteousness. Peter says we are His own special people. We're a part of God's own. We're special in the eyes of God. Each one of us is special in the eyes of God.

Now, what are we supposed to do with this? It is so "that you may proclaim the praises of Him who called you out of darkness into His marvelous light" (1 Peter 2:9 NKJV). God did all of this to equip us and anoint us to be a light shining out into the darkness. The Message Bible says it this way, "But you are the ones chosen by God, chosen for the high calling of priestly work, chosen to be a holy people, God's instruments to do his work and speak out for him, to tell others of the night-and-day difference he made for you" (1 Peter 2:9 MSG). We are to tell others of the night-and-day difference He made for us—that brings it down for the entire church. We all have a testimony.

When we begin to preach about taking the gospel out to the world, if we preach it from the Great Commission, then everybody thinks it's just the apostle, prophet, evangelist, pastor, and teacher. But the apostle Peter breaks it down and says that every one of us can go out and tell the difference that God has done in our life. When we're living in the light, we're walking in the light, we're living as a royal priest to God, we're living as one who is serving the Lord. Then that light shines out and people say, "What is it that's different about you?" All of a sudden, you take the revival that has taken place in you and share it with them. True revival is not just us experiencing who we are in Christ, but it is sharing with others who are around us.

You may think, "I don't know how to preach." You don't have to know how to preach; do you know how to talk? Just go ahead and talk in your own language. Peter says we're to share these things and give out these things.

In this part of the book, we're talking about revival and having a passion for the harvest, passion to reach our world and to do the part that God has called us to do. In Matthew 5, the Lord Jesus was teaching on what we call the Beatitudes. He was teaching the people how to live. He was teaching them how to walk in an ungodly world and how to live for Him. In verse 14, He says, "You are the light of the world. A city that is set on a hill cannot be hidden. Nor do they light a lamp and put it under a basket, but on a lampstand, and it gives light to all who are in the house" (Matthew 5:14-15 NKJV).

Notice that He said you are the light of the world. He didn't say you're the light in the church. We're living in a dark world and you're the light, the one that's to glow. You're the one that's to bring enlightenment. You're the one, in your life and in your lifestyle, in your words and how you live, you are to be a light shining out to the world that's in darkness.

In other words, He says, "Listen, if you're going to really live for me, you can't hide it." You don't go to church on Sunday morning, give your heart to the Lord, and then sneak around all week hoping nobody finds out at the job that you are no longer a sinner, but now you're one of them holy-rollers. You're not going to survive if you're ashamed of what happened to you at the altar of the Lord Jesus Christ. The Lord says you're not to be a light that gets lit and then hidden under a basket.

Here's what you do. He says you're to be on a lampstand and you're to give light to all who are in the house. He's saying you're to demonstrate with your life. You're to be a light in the world. You're a light around the people you work with. You're a light in your home. You're a light in your community with your lifestyle, your attitude, your praise, your thanksgiving, your service to the Lord. It becomes a light shining to those who are around you and you put it up and you're not ashamed of Jesus Christ nor of His gospel. And you rise up and you say, "Praise God. I'm not going to act like darkness because I'm light. I'm not going to talk like darkness because I'm light. I'm not going to live like darkness because I'm light. I'm not going to go where darkness is, where people are living and doing the dark things. I'm going to walk in the light." You put it on. That means I'm not ashamed of the decision that I made for Jesus Christ.

I believe that we're either ashamed of our decision for Jesus Christ or the devil has hoodwinked us and got us so fearful of what they're going to say about us. We're not willing to let anybody see it. The Lord says, "Listen, you are light and you're to live like light. You're not to hide your light. You're not to be afraid of what people are going to say about it. In fact, you're supposed to be a light in the darkness. When they're cussing, you're praising. When they're talking doubt, you're talking faith. When they're talking failure, you're talking victory. When they're talking like they're not going to make it, you're talking as an overcomer. When they say, 'I don't know what we're going to do,' you say, 'Let's pray.'" You don't have to be a preacher to do that. You have to be somebody that's on fire and somebody that's got revival and anointing and you're a light for Jesus Christ. When we begin to walk in the light of His life and let it shine through us. We don't have to go in and just be hard and be critical; that's not what light does. Light comes in and dispels the darkness. Light just says, "Hey, let me help you see all the blessings the Lord has for you."

We've got to get rid of fear. The devil's lied to us in our minds about what people might say. We've got to get ourselves to the place where we absolutely are convicted and passionate about the decision that we've made to live for Jesus. You've got to get that way and you've got to praise Him.

I remember John Osteen, Joel Osteen's dad, and he used to say he was a big man. He was about five-eight, but he said he was big on the inside. One time he was on the elevator and he was as bold as a lion, just bold and on fire for God. He was a Baptist filled with the Holy Ghost. A guy on the elevator was just cussing away, about every other word. They made it about three floors with him cussing and finally, Pastor John just threw up his hands and started saying, "Oh hallelujah. Thank you, Jesus. Praise you, Lord; glory to God. Thank you." The guy jumped back and looked at him and said, "What are you doing?" He said, "I demand equal time. You curse Him. I praise Him." He just released the light of God in that place.

We've got to come to that place. We've got to get to the place where we are so excited and so passionate, so determined that our decision is the right decision that whatever is going on around us doesn't bother us. My love for Jesus is what motivates me.

Jesus continues, "Let your light so shine before men, that they may see your good works and glorify your Father in heaven" (Matthew 5:16 NKJV). Good works mean you are living, acting, talking, and being like the Lord Jesus Christ. Every one of us is going to be faced with an opportunity, whether you've put a basket over your light or you put it on a lampstand somewhere in your life, you're going to have to come to a place that when you become challenged and you have to make a decision to let the light of the dedication you made to the Lord shine.

I remember it happening to me not too long after I'd given my heart to the Lord. I was going to East Tennessee State University and playing ball. This was even before Bonnie and I had got married and I was on fire for God. I'd made a commitment to the Lord. In fact, we'd made a decision to get married, but I'd been running around with the guys and drinking and doing some stuff I shouldn't have been doing. Just being basically a sinner like them. Then I gave my heart totally to the Lord. I was all excited about Jesus.

One of the guys who was on the football team came to me not long after I had given my life to Jesus and said, "Hey, we're going to have a keg party over at such-and-such's house on Friday night, come on out. We're going to have a party; it's going to be great." I said, "Well, now I can't do it." He looked at me like something was strange, thinking, "What's wrong with this guy? He's been there before." He said, "Well, come on over. It won't cost you anything. If you can just come on, just have a party with us." I said, "I don't drink."

He was bold; he came and grabbed my chin, pulled my mouth down, and said, "It looks like it's still open. Surely you can." Now, I wasn't filled with the Holy Ghost at the time, but I had the witness of the Spirit in me. I was born of the Spirit. Down on the inside, I heard this: "If he's going to be that bold for the devil, what are you going to do?" I just stepped back. And I said, "Well, listen, my mouth is still open, and I can still swallow. But I just gave my heart to the Lord Jesus Christ. And I've been saved and I don't need to drink that. I don't need to have that. I'm a child of God now. I've been set free. You want to go to church with me on Sunday?" He jumped back and looked at me. He said I'll see you and took off.

Every one of us is going to come to a place like that. Until you decide to take the shade off of your lamp and the basket off your lamp and go ahead and shine, the enemy will keep you defeated. You will not walk in the reviving power of God Almighty in your life. Somewhere down the line, you've got to take a stand and know that you are a child of God, that you're not ashamed of that decision, that you're going to heaven. Jesus is your Lord and you are God's very own special person. You're going to begin to let the Lord work in you and through you to tell the people the difference that He has done in changing your night into day. God will bless you; He sees us through those works.

Acts 2 is really a great example of the revival in the church, showing how the church is to operate in that revival and maintain the revival. We know that in Acts 2, there were 120 in the upper room. They all got filled with the Holy Ghost. They spoke in other tongues, began to get drunk in the Spirit, and excited in God. It went right out of the upper room right out in the street. When there's a true revival, you can't hold it inside of a building. So, they went out and people were wondering what was going on.

If you'll get on fire for God, people will drive from miles around to see you burn. Now nobody's going to come along if you're melting. You can take a block of ice, six by six feet, put it in your front yard. Nobody will come by to see it melt, but you can take two or three old tires, put some gas on them, and light the fire and they'll come from all over the place. Fire trucks will come. Police will come. Neighbors will come to ask, "What is burning in their yard?" When the church gets on fire and the smoke of the Holy Ghost is rising up all around us, they're going to come from all around to find out what is burning and ask, "What's going on in that place?" God is wanting to ignite that fire and bring the light into each and every one of us.

In Acts 2, after that fire is brought out to the people, Peter stands up and he preaches a powerful message. He preaches about what God's going to do in these last days, that He is going to pour out His spirit. Peter preaches about how Jesus Christ was the son of God and the son of David. He preaches about how Jesus came, died on the cross, and was buried. Peter tells how at the hand of

God, Jesus was raised up from the dead and that He is the Lord Christ that God Almighty sent to be the Messiah. Peter is preaching this gospel and you drop down to verse 37: "Now, when they heard this, they were cut to the heart, and said to Peter and the rest of the apostles, 'Men and brethren, what shall we do?'" (NKJV).

Our lives have to be so on fire for God and so lit up with the light of the life of God that people say, "What do I need to do to have what you have?" We have to maintain the fire. We have to keep our lamps full of oil. That's why in Acts 1:8, He said that you need the Holy Ghost so the power of God is constantly in you so you can be that witness. That's why we saw in Psalm 92:10 that you need to be anointed with fresh oil every day. That's why we saw in Ephesians 5:18 that we need to be stirred and stimulated with the Holy Ghost, continually filled, stirred, and stimulated with the Holy Ghost so that we are constantly on fire for God and excited for God and our life provokes people to want to come to see what we have.

We each need to make a decision that I'm going to be bolder for Jesus than the sinner is for the devil. The kingdom of God is going to be more on display in my life than the kingdom of darkness is in the world. I'm going to live this thing. I'm all in.

Next, Peter answers them. "Then Peter said to them, 'Repent and let every one of you be baptized in the name of Jesus Christ for the remission of sins; and you shall receive the gift of the Holy Spirit. For the promise is to you and to your children, and to all who are afar off, as many as the Lord our God will call'" (Acts 2:38-39 NKJV). He taught about getting born again and then receiving the gift of the Holy Spirit, which is the baptism of the Holy Spirit.

"With many other words, he testified and exhorted them, saying, 'Be saved from this perverse generation'" (Acts 2:40 NKJV). In other words, he's telling them, "Don't let this opportunity go by. See for yourself. Turn to God; let God do a work in your life." That's passion. That's a revived man. That's an awakened man. That's a person who's full of the Holy Ghost letting his light shine. He's not ashamed of the gospel. He's preaching to the very people that yelled "Crucify!" just fifty days earlier. Here he is ministering to them in boldness because he's all in for Jesus. That's revival.

Look what happened next. "Then those who gladly received his word were baptized; and that day about three thousand souls were added to them" (Acts 2:41 NKJV). Quit letting the devil lie to you and say that people will mock you and persecute you and come against you if you tell them about Jesus. Maybe one out of ten will be obnoxious to you. But what about the nine that you planted good seed into? Many of us won't share what's going on in our life because we think somebody's going to get in our faces. They're not going to get in your face. They gladly received the word that Peter was sharing with them and they were baptized. They just went from 120 in that church to 3,120 in a church. That was worth about seven days of fasting and praying in the upper room. Now they were in revival, and people wanted in on what God was doing and they wanted to see what God was doing and they wanted to experience it in their lives.

We have to understand something: the early church made Pentecost a movement, not a one-time experience. We talk about Pentecost and we leave it there: the day of Pentecost. But the apostle Peter said these are the things that are going to happen in the last days. What he's talking about here is this: don't make Pentecost just an event that took place one time in your life. Make Pentecost a continual work in your life; showing that Jesus is Lord is a movement that took place in your life. On the day of Pentecost, they didn't have a religious day; they started a movement called revival and the church began to grow and from a handful of people who were on fire for God and that were all in for Jesus began a movement that changed the world.

If they could do that in Jerusalem, we can do it in our cities. But it takes a group that's not ashamed of the gospel. Those who see themselves as light and take the shade off their lamp and put it on a stand and say, "Lord, let anybody who wants to see, let them see what you've done for me and let them know you'll do it for them."

We become bold and sold out and committed to that which Jesus told us to do.

Let me show you a few things that are going to happen here with this early church because they kept that revival going. This is what happens when true revival breaks loose: "And they continued steadfastly in the apostles' doctrine and fellowship, in the breaking of bread, and in prayers" (Acts 2:42 NKJV). These three thousand kept the revival going by keeping their personal walk with Jesus alive and well. They stayed on fire for God. They got together. They prayed, they stayed in the word. They just continually developed themselves. They didn't just have a one-day experience, a Sunday morning experience. They had a continuous experience, and they continued to press into God.

This book will have been a failure if you get excited for a few days, but by Sunday, you're back down to the mundane, going-through-the-motions Christianity that we had before. This has got to be a thing where we continue to walk in this. We continue to hunger for the Word. We continue to lean into the Spirit. We continue to break bread. We continue to build ourselves up and stay full of the Holy Ghost and fire.

"Then fear came upon every soul, and many wonders and signs were done through the apostles" (Acts 2:43 NKJV). He is saying here that they had powerful, anointed church services because they had great respect and reverence for the things of God. They stopped taking for granted salvation. They stopped taking for granted the mercy of God. They stopped taking for granted the grace of God. They stopped taking for granted the Holy Word of God. They stopped taking for granted that they spoke in tongues one time and God blessed them. They kept it fresh and alive and powerful in their lives. When they came together, it was a celebration of Jesus and a celebration of God. They came together and mighty services took place because they came in fired up. They kept everything fresh and alive.

"Now all who believed were together, and had all things common" (Acts 2:44 NKJV). They brought unity into the church.

They stayed united together. They refused to let any kind of division get in the church. You shouldn't be telling somebody else what you heard about somebody else. You should be going to them and saying, "I heard this. Is it true? Let's pray about it and take care of it." But you shouldn't be gossiping and causing division in the church. The early Christians kept unity in the church. They defended one another in the church. They refused to let the devil come in through trickery, treachery, lies, and deceptions and pull people down. If somebody was struggling with problems, they would go help them out.

We know because later on when Peter and John got in trouble, they all got together and had an all-night prayer meeting for them. They stayed together because they wanted a movement of God. You can't have a movement of God winning the lost when you're attacking each other. We've got to make a decision. We're all in this together, and we're not all perfect. We're not all mature. We're not all fully grown. I've got flaws. You've got flaws.

I can remember the first time I kind of saw that about myself. I was praying about somebody to come in, and I said, "Well, Lord, I'd like to have him. But you know, he's got some quirks." The Lord spoke to me and said, "Well, you've got quirks." I said to the Lord, Oh my God, I've got quirks. Oh, Jesus help me." So, I quit judging everybody else's quirks. I found out that none of us have it all together. We should look beyond the faults and love each other and help each other grow in the things of God and choose to be united as a body of believers, lifting each other up and with a common cause: to bring the gospel of the kingdom to every person that we can possibly reach in our life.

Then we find out: "[They] sold their possessions and goods, and divided them among all, as anyone had need" (Acts 2:45 NKJV). They were givers. They bought into the vision. They supported the vision. That doesn't mean that they all just had everything. It just means that they were taking things and sowing, and they wanted this preaching to go forth. They wanted the gospel to be shared and the church to prosper and they wanted people's needs to be met and they wanted to be a part of it. In other words, they partnered with a vision and sowed into it. You've got to get involved even with your finances and even with your talents and abilities and everything about you; you've got to get into it. If this bothers you, you need to get refilled with the Holy Ghost? If you were full of the Holy Ghost, you wouldn't get all upset about that. You would say, "Woo, glory to God. I get to be a part of this." The Spirit of God would draw you right into that.

Paul says that in Galatians 5: "Flesh lusts against the Spirit, and the Spirit against the flesh; and these are contrary to one another, so that you do not do the things that you wish" (v 17 NKJV). If you're walking in the flesh, you can't please God. Thank God that flesh has been crucified and you can walk in the Spirit. If you walk in the Spirit, you will fulfill all the things God's asked you to do. If your flesh rises up, then you have got to crucify the flesh and say, "God help me overcome this."

We're talking about being all-in, sold out for God. That's just part of it. Look what it says in verse 46. "So, continuing daily with one accord in the temple, and breaking bread from house to house, they ate their food with gladness and simplicity of heart" (Acts 2:46 NKJV). In other words, they just kept it simple: love God, stay faithful, praise God. Notice here that they had a constant revival. They lived their Christianity in their church, in their personal life, and in their public life. Daily, they lived and broke bread in their homes. They fellowshipped in their homes. They prayed with each other. They saw each other on the street and stopped and fellowshipped. Then when it came time for church, they were in church. Revival has to be a daily, twenty-four/seven thing.

I love seeing Jesus in our lives. That's what brings revival. That's why you have to have the Holy Spirit because you can't do these things without being filled with the Holy Spirit. You can't live this way without the Holy Spirit. You can't do it. You can't just take my word for it; take the word of the Bible. In Zechariah 4, in the Old Testament, God is speaking to Zerubbabel and He basically tells him, "Hey, listen, you're going to rebuild the temple. You're going to lay the foundation. You're going to raise it up. Your hand started it and your hands are going to finish it. But I've got a word for you. It's not going to be by your might, nor by your power, but by my Spirit, you're going to get this thing done. And if you try to do it in your power and your might, you're going to fail. So, you have to have my anointing upon your life because it's my Spirit that's going to empower you to get this thing done."

Going back to Acts 2, the final verse says they were "praising God and having favor with all the people. And the Lord added to the church daily those who were being saved" (Acts 2:47 NKJV). Notice that they kept an attitude of gratitude. They had favor with all the people, not just with the Christians. Even those who haven't seen the light yet may all of a sudden start doing good things for you. When you walk off the guy will say, "I don't know why I did it for that Christian. I don't know how I gave them a deal. How did I do that? I never do that." But God was giving them favor with all people.

They were living this thing, God's revival was taking place, and they were letting their light shine. They had got their lamp. They were a light up on a lampstand. They were letting their good works be seen. They had got an attitude of praise and they were staying simple. They were not trying to think more highly of themselves. They were just loving God and loving people and letting the Word work. They were forgiven people and the joy of the Lord was their strength as they walked with God. God was blessing and moving and manifesting Himself. The whole city was happy because they were blessing them. We should be blessers and not cursers. We should be speaking good things and releasing good things and not being a part of the bad.

God was adding daily those who were being saved. People were constantly being saved because when revival is going on, people get saved at the grocery store parking lot. People get saved down here at the mall; people get saved around the neighborhood; people get saved over at the ball field. People get saved wherever you're at because the anointing of God's on you, not just in the sanctuary, but it's on your life. When you are walking around loving God and being a part of it, somebody is going to come up with a need, to have a prayer.

I can remember one time I was playing basketball over at the YMCA back years ago. We'd been playing about three games, and our team was pretty good that day. We were shutting everybody down, and I came down from a rebound and my ankle turned and it popped. And a couple of guys turned their heads and they said, "Oh, we heard that." I'm lying there, and I felt like the top of my head went off. They're all looking at me. I said, "Listen, I need to pray and I need to pray right now. If you can believe God with me, then join your faith. If you can't, just turn your back and look the other way. Because I ain't got time to play with you." I laid hands on my ankle and I prayed for God's healing. I prayed in tongues. I worshiped God and I was praying to the Lord. All of a sudden, the anointing of God hit my ankle and I jumped up and started walking around and those guys looked at me.

About six months later, I walked into a business. I didn't know this guy who'd been playing basketball was one of the businessmen downtown. But I walked in and he said, "I'll never forget that afternoon we were playing ball. That's the wildest thing I ever saw in my life." I proceeded to witness to him.

Another day, I was over there playing, and all of a sudden, this guy comes over and he said, "Could you come here?" I said, "Well, I'm playing." He said, "Get somebody else." So I got someone else to fill in and I walked over to the water fountain. He said, " I am so sick. I'm feeling so bad." He didn't go to church here, but he knew I was a pastor. He said, "Would you lay your hands on me and pray?" I laid hands on him and prayed. He got filled with the Holy Ghost and just started praising God, and God healed him right there at the water fountain.

One day I was on the first tee at Sugarwood Golf Course with my friend. We had just hit our drives, and we're getting ready to leave. My friend said, "Pastor, is that somebody calling your name?" We could hear it but couldn't tell where it was coming from. We looked around, and from about three fairways over, a guy in a golf cart was driving like he's crazy. I could see him kind of swelling up. I said, "What is it?" He was a Christian. He said, "I got stung by a bee and I'm deadly allergic to it. I'm not going to be able to get to the doctor. I said, 'God, what am I going to do?' I looked up and saw you standing over here. Now the Lord said, 'Go have Brother Huffman lay his hands on you.'" Then he said, "Lay your hands on me right now. I'm going to die." I laid hands on him. We prayed, and I laid hands on him and ministered to him. The symptoms left within the next five minutes, and he was praising God. He lived for about another fifteen years, and all over this region, he'd tell people about how God healed him out on the golf course that day he got stung.

God doesn't just use me. He said, "These signs shall follow them that believe." This is the believers' lifestyle. This is how we're supposed to live, but you have got to be full of the Holy Ghost, living for the Lord, praising Him, serving the Lord, and magnifying His name. You have to keep your lamp full of oil so that the light shines bright.

Remember that in Acts 3, Peter and John went up to the temple in the evening to pray. They saw a lame man, and they got him healed. They were preaching to the people and the religious leaders threw them in jail overnight. The next day, they brought them before the tribunal and they began to ask, "What are you doing? How'd you get this done?" Peter, then filled with the Holy Ghost, began to preach to them and the anointing came on him.

In Acts 4:13, it says, "Now when they saw the boldness of Peter and John, and perceived that they were uneducated and untrained men, they marveled. And they realized that they had been with Jesus" (NKJV). The key I want you to see is this. The leaders saw the boldness: where did they get that boldness? The Holy Ghost came on Peter and the boldness of God rose up on the inside of him. In other words, the anointing gives us boldness to answer the questions, answer the charges, and speak out for the Lord even when people don't want to hear it.

If you don't have the anointing of the Holy Ghost operating in you, when they began to challenge you, to try to shut you up and tell you to be quiet, you'll cower down, and the spirit of fear will come on you and you'll give up. But when you're anointed with the Holy Ghost, and they try to get you to shut up and be quiet, the revival fire of God will burn and your lamp will glow and you'll rise up and speak truth. It was so powerful on Peter that they let them go. But they said, "We're going to let you go. But don't you preach anymore in the name of Jesus." Peter basically said, "You just go ahead and judge what you think is right. Should we obey you? Or should we obey God?"

Here's what happened next: "And being let go, they went to their own companions and reported all that the chief priests and the elders had said to them" (Acts 4:23 NKJV). When they were let go, they went home but not to backslide and stop going to church anymore because the rulers were offended because they're trying to witness for the Lord. You don't let persecution, obstacles, somebody saying something bad toward you, or challenging your faith to cause you to fall away from God or not go to church. That's when you run into the church. Don't let persecution make you run out of the church. That persecution should run you into the church. When there's revival, we refuse to let offenses keep us from being in the church.

The harder the devil attacks, the more I'm in church; the more people that stand against me, the more I'm in church. When Peter and John reported this, the church got together and they started praying. They don't start off with, "God, help me please." "So, when they heard that, they raised their voice to God with one accord and said, 'Lord, You are God, who made the heaven and earth and the sea, and all that is in them'" (Acts 4:24 NKJV). When the enemy is attacking you and trying to put out your fire, you need to go to the Lord and say, "Lord, you are God. Not them. Not the problem. You are God, you have the final say, you're the greater one. You're going to take care of me. I don't care how bad it looks. You're God. I don't care how hard they're coming against me. Lord, you're God. God, everything was made by and for you. You're over everything. God, there's nothing too big that you can't handle. There's nothing too great that I'm facing that you can't get me through." That's basically what the church did. They went back and bragged on God and reminded themselves how great God was and reminded themselves why they were doing this. Why am I out here putting myself on the line to be mocked, ridiculed, or threatened? Because I have the revelation of the Lord Jesus Christ abiding in my life.

Revelation has got me through many scrapes. That revelation has kept me on fire for God. That revelation has kept me from falling away from the Lord. God has got me through times when Bonnie and I didn't know where the next meal was going to come from or how we were going to get gas to get home after we preached the gospel to the church. When Joshua was just a little guy and he was struggling with fevers, we didn't have any health insurance. We didn't have any money. We were preaching at a little old church. I remember Bonnie was up with him till midnight. I took him from midnight. I sat in a rocking chair and prayed in the Spirit. He just wallowed in my arms and I worshiped God. About four o'clock in the morning, he just went cool and laid his head in my lap. I just thank God he was healed. What got me through that? Lord, you are God.

If you get the revelation that Jesus is Lord and Lord, you are God—no matter what's coming against me, Lord, you're God, and I'm in this because of that—then there's nothing impossible.

The church began to worship Him and praise Him and magnify Him because they refused to let any kind of attack of the enemy steal their revival or fire out of their life. The whole church reminded themselves of the greatness of God. Now they're going to ask this great God to get involved with them. They say, "Lord, look on their threats, and grant to Your servants that with all boldness, they may speak your word" (Acts 4:29 NKJV). In other words, the more they attack, give us that much more boldness, Lord. The harder it gets, give me that much more courage, Lord. When it gets to the place they don't want to hear me talking about you anymore, give me the boldness and the courage to say something else. You let me speak your word.

Then look what they do. They just don't want to speak the Word. They want the power to flow out of what they're saying. They say, "Lord, we don't only just want to talk about you." They ask that "by stretching forth Your hand to heal, and that signs and wonders may be done through the name of Your holy Servant Jesus" (Acts 4:30 NKJV). In other words, "Lord, the authorities are telling us not to get any more people healed. But Lord, I'm asking you that right in the midst of persecution anoint us so that we can see your mighty hand move and lives will be changed. Lord, give me more boldness and courage to be a greater influence for you. Let me love those who are coming against me. Let me have boldness to speak right into their face. Not to get back at them, but to let them know that this is the truth."

I'm going to keep saying it to you. I'm going to keep living it, and we'll let Jesus be Lord of it all. Then we see God's response in verse 31: "And when they had prayed, the place where they were assembled together was shaken; and they were all filled with the Holy Spirit, and they spoke the word of God with boldness" (Acts 4:31 NKJV).

This is the three thousand who got saved and filled with the Holy Ghost just a couple of chapters before. This isn't the baptism of the Holy Spirit. This is a fresh anointing of the Holy Spirit. This is already a Spirit-filled church, but they got filled again with a fresh anointing. When they got filled with a fresh anointing, they spoke the Word of God with boldness. If you're not speaking the Word of God with confidence and boldness, you know what you need. You need to ask God to fill you with a fresh anointing of the Holy Spirit because the power to be a witness comes from the Holy Spirit, according to Jesus in Acts 1:8: "You shall receive power when the Holy Spirit has come upon you; and you shall be witnesses to Me" (NKJV). If I'm losing my boldness, I need a fresh anointing of the Holy Ghost. I don't need another baptism; I just need to go to the Lord and say, "Lord, anoint me with fresh oil; fill me up and cause me to overflow because I'm taking this home with me and I'm going to take it to school tomorrow. I'm going to take it on the job tomorrow, and I'll take it out in my leisure tomorrow, and I'll take it to my friends tomorrow, and I'll take it to my enemies tomorrow. Lord, in fact, I'm going to live this every day the rest of this week. On Sunday morning, I'm going to come in to church and we're going to have a time in the Lord because we're all going to come in here expecting the hand of God to move and the Holy Ghost to fall." We're going to come and celebrate our victories. Whether they've totally manifested or they're on their way, we're going to celebrate victory because we refused to lose, because Lord, you are God.

CPSIA information can be obtained
at www.ICGtesting.com
Printed in the USA
LVHW011341030422
715110LV00005B/8